Meet Your Matcha

60 delicious ways to cook, serve, drink and eat matcha

Jassy Davis &
Erin Niimi Longhurst

HarperCollins*Publishers*
1 London Bridge Street
London SE1 9GF
WilliamCollinsBooks.com

HarperCollins*Publishers*
Macken House, 39/40 Mayor Street Upper,
Dublin 1, D01 C9W8, Ireland

First published by HarperCollins*Publishers* in 2026

1 3 5 7 9 10 8 6 4 2

Text copyright © Jassy Davis and Erin Niimi Longhurst 2026
Copyright © HarperCollins*Publishers* 2026

Written by Jassy Davis and Erin Niimi Longhurst

Design by e-Digital Design
Publishing Director: Caitlin Doyle
Production Controller: Alan Cracknell
Images: Pages 127 and 161 Adobe Stock. All other images Shutterstock

Jassy Davis and Erin Niimi Longhurst assert their moral right to be identified as the authors of this work.

All rights reserved. No parts of this publication may be reproduced, stored in a retrieval system, or transmitted, in any form or by any means, electronic, mechanical, photocopying, recording, or otherwise, without the prior permission of the publishers.

Without limiting the author's and publisher's exclusive rights, any unauthorised use of this publication to train generative artificial intelligence (AI) technologies is expressly prohibited. HarperCollins also exercise their rights under Article 4(3) of the Digital Single Market Directive 2019/790 and expressly reserve this publication from the text and data mining exception.

A catalogue record for this book is available from the British Library.
Library of Congress Cataloging-in Details have been applied for.

ISBN 978-0-00-882205-7

All reasonable efforts have been made by the author and publishers to trace the copyright owners of the material quoted in this book and of any images reproduced in this book. In the event that the author or publishers are notified of any mistakes or omissions by copyright owners after publication, the author and publishers will endeavour to rectify the position accordingly for any subsequent printing.

Printed and bound in Latvia

CONTENTS

INTRODUCTION 4
Welcome 5
Harvest 6
Health 14
Heritage 21
History 32

CHOOSING AND PREPARING MATCHA 40

RECIPES 52
Drinks 54
Breakfasts 92
Baking 116
Desserts 156

Index 176

INTRODUCTION

WELCOME

A 21st-century icon that's centuries old; nothing sums up modern life quite like a cup of matcha.

For many years barely anyone outside of Japan had heard of matcha. But in the last 15 years, as more people have travelled to and from Japan, matcha has travelled with them. Initially as a representative of Japan's ancient cultural traditions. Then as a health food that might work miracles on our minds and bodies. And, finally, as a social media superstar. If you're on Instagram or TikTok, you already know what an iced matcha latte looks like. Social platforms are where many of us first learned about matcha, and where we share pictures of our favourite matcha-flavoured foods and drinks.

Whether you're a matcha expert or simply matcha curious, this book will help you enjoy this legendary green tea. Discover the culture and history behind Japan's most famous drink. Learn how to buy matcha and prepare a simple bowl of *usucha*. Then enjoy over 60 matcha-infused recipes.

You'll find trending drinks, like Strawberry Matcha Latte (page 58) and Matcha Mojito (page 86), as well as healthy breakfasts such as Matcha & Coconut Chia Pudding (page 97), Matcha & Coconut Bliss Balls (page 111), and Matcha Overnight Oats (page 101).

Increasingly popular as an ingredient, matcha has made its way into all kinds of baked goods, snacks, and treats. Whether you like French–Japanese fusion patisserie, like Matcha Financiers (page 152), indulgent American bakes such as Marbled Matcha Cheesecake Brownies (page 136), or timeless classics like Matcha & Raspberry Swiss Roll (page 150), you'll find something indulgent to suit your tastebuds.

Full of practical advice and written with love and passion for all things matcha, this cookbook will help you make the most of our favourite powdered green tea.

HARVEST

Matcha has a distinctive colour and flavour that is unlike that of any other type of tea, due to the unique way in which it is cultivated and harvested. These characteristics are strictly protected – defined by bodies such as the International Organization for Standardization, and the Japan Tea Central Public Interest Incorporated Association. To be classified as a 'matcha', the tea must be derived from the *Camellia sinensis* tea plant; it must be grown under cover of shade; it must be steamed and dried; and it must be finely milled or ground into a powder. (This is the literal translation of the word matcha, referring to the ground, powdered tea form.)

The complex production method behind matcha is the main reason why it is such an expensive product. It is a delicate process, where the timing, location, and method of collection are integral and ever-evolving – precision is key, as there is very little margin for error. However, while the process might be expensive, this method of preservation means that many health benefits of matcha can be attributed to it – by capturing the plant at the height of its freshness, a lot of the goodness and health benefits espoused by matcha's biggest fans are passed through into the body in this way. By steaming the *tencha* leaves (the term used to refer to leaves before they are ground into a fine powder) to capture their vibrant pigment, the plant's high levels of chlorophyll, amino acids, vitamins, and minerals are maintained at their peak as well.

KEY MATCHA REGIONS

In the same way that climate, soil, and topography can produce a distinctive flavour of grape, and therefore wine, the way in which the environment shapes matcha varies from region to region. The key places where matcha is produced in Japan include Uji, near Kyoto, Nishio in Aichi Prefecture, Shizuoka Prefecture, as well as Kagoshima. (See page 42 for the impact of regions on matcha flavour and quality.)

KYOTO (UJI)

SHIZUOKA

AICHI (NISHIO)

KAGOSHIMA

GROWTH & HARVEST

1. **Shading the plants:** The distinctive green colour of matcha is a result of the *Camellia sinensis* tea leaves being grown in the shade for at least three to four weeks before the plant is harvested (usually in April). Shading the plant increases chlorophyll production, as well as the potency of the L-theanine amino acid in matcha (the benefits of which are outlined in the health section of this book, on pages 14–20).

2. **First flush – *shincha* or *ichibancha*:** The first flush or harvest, known as *shincha* ('new tea') or *ichibancha* ('first tea') is the most prized and therefore the most sought-after for tea ceremonies, due to its taste – and this is often reflected in the price of the product. Often harvested in late April or early May, the leaves are bright green, delicate, and smooth – the best quality with a relatively short harvesting window to preserve freshness. This is often referred to as 'ceremonial grade'. *Tencha* leaves can be hand-picked or machine-harvested – the former is often preferable to tea ceremony practitioners, but result in a much more expensive product overall, as the process is more labour-intensive.

3. **Second flush – *nibancha*:** For the second harvest, or *nibancha*, the *tencha* leaves are harvested in June and July. By now the leaves are bigger and have a slightly more bitter taste than the first harvest, but they are still suitable for daily drinking and would work well in everyday lattes and drinks. This is often referred to as premium or culinary-grade matcha.

4. **Third flush – *sanbancha*:** The third harvest takes place in late summer and early autumn, by which time the plant will have had some sun exposure, which results in leaves that have a more bitter taste and a browner colour. These might eventually become *hojicha*-style green tea. *Hojicha* is roasted, giving it a nutty aroma. This results in lower caffiene, which makes it a popular choice for after dinner. Because it is roasted, a lower grade tea leaf (like *sanbancha*) is often used.

5. **Fourth and final flush – *yonbancha* or *shuutoubancha* (known as autumn/winter tea):** A fourth flush takes place to prune and maintain the plant for next year's harvest, but these leaves are not often consumed because of the lower quality of the product.

INTRODUCTION **9**

PROCESS & PACKAGING

Once the plant has been picked, things move quickly. Only the greenest and youngest parts of the plant are cultivated first – this raw tea stage is referred to as *namacha* – which is done to prevent oxidation to the plant. Timing is key at this stage; the leaves must be packaged, processed, and sealed with as quick a turnaround as possible to preserve the freshness of the tea and ensure the *tencha* retains its vibrant green colour.

As the tea is picked, it is steamed the same day in a rough form (known as *aracha*) to preserve the beneficial nutrients of the whole leaf. Next, it is shifted and sorted, and the steamed *tencha* leaves are then dried and later ground into a fine powder. Unlike other types of green tea varieties, where dried leaves are steeped in water to form the beverage, with matcha the whole plant (in its ground, powdered form) is consumed, making its effects more potent.

The different schools of tea will have their own blends, combining different leaves from various plants to maintain a uniform flavour profile. The *tencha* leaves are stoneground to be as fine as possible, becoming the matcha powder we are now familiar with.

Particularly for the first-flush *ichibancha* tea, preserving its hue and aroma is crucial, and therefore any further oxidation that could dull the flavour and colour needs to be prevented as much as possible. Matcha teas are often served and sold in dark tin containers and caddies, vacuum-packed for freshness, and are best kept cool. For this reason, matcha, once opened, should be used while the flavour and colour are intact, as the way the tea is processed essentially suspends and preserves it at its height. Unlike a fine wine, matcha doesn't get better with age, so if you are lucky enough to get your hands on a tin of first-flush *ichibancha*, it is better to appreciate it at its peak rather than have it sit at the back of a cupboard for years waiting for a special occasion.

HARVESTING TECHNIQUES: HAND-PICKED VS MACHINE-PICKED

Tea leaves are harvested either manually (*te-tsumi*) or by machine. The premium-quality, ceremonial-grade matchas are more likely to be hand-picked, due to the attention and care required for teas of this kind, whereas the lower-grade teas will more often than not be machine-picked, as quality cannot be assured in the same way. The hand-picking process also results in less product damage overall, but it is, understandably, far more time-consuming than machine-harvesting methods.

MATCHA CULTIVARS

Cultivated varieties (also known as cultivars) of matcha are known for their differing flavour profiles, as you might find with certain grape varieties in wine – each has its own flavour, aroma, texture, and differences in pigmentation. Climate, harvest, and processing influence the umami, acidity, and sweetness of the matcha varieties. Different schools of teas might have their own blends of cultivars – as with honeys

that have been blended from various sources, the single-source cultivar matchas tend to be more expensive due to their purity.

- **Yabukita:** The most commonly grown variety (over 70 per cent of matcha is this variety), used in ceremonial matcha (particularly *koicha*: thick tea) – the plant is hardy to grow and produces a tea that is rich in umami.
- **Samidori:** Grown in Kyoto, it is a sweeter variety with a brighter hue than some others, making it ideal for thin, *usucha*-style teas.
- **Okumidori:** A variety that is harvested later, with a more robust (slightly bitter) feel, making it ideal for blends.
- **Gokou:** A relatively new cultivar, it is bold but sought-after, due to its rarity.
- **Asahi:** A light and bright variety with no bitterness, Asahi also lends itself well to being blended with other cultivars for complexity.
- **Saemidori:** Another more recent variety that is sweet and smooth with a light colour.

Different *tenchas* are blended and curated by tea masters, merchants, and experts before they are ground and milled into a fine powder to become the matcha that is then canned, vacuum-sealed, and sold for tea ceremonies or wider consumption.

'Meanwhile, let us have a sip of tea. The afternoon glow is brightening the bamboo, the fountains are bubbling with delight, the soughing of the pines is heard in our kettle. Let us dream of evanescence, and linger in the beautiful foolishness of things.'
—Okakura Kakuzo

THE TEA OF THE 'HACHIJU HACHIYA' - THE 88TH DAY AND NIGHT

The eighty-eighth day, or *hachiju hachiya,* after the beginning of spring (which is said to start in early February) marks the beginning of the harvest season, when farmers could be confident that they would be able to avoid any sudden frost or cold snaps that might hinder their crop. It is considered an auspicious time to brew a cup of matcha, as it is believed that drinking tea made from leaves plucked on that night (around the time of *ichibancha* – the first flush) will make the drinker live a long and prosperous life. Tea festivals are held on this day, too. The *shincha* – 'new tea' – of the eighty-eighth night was said to be full of vitality that could be passed along to the drinker, which made it sought-after to fuel a busy (and successful, one hoped) harvest season ahead.

> *'Tea is a work of art and needs a master hand to bring out its noblest qualities.'*
> — Okakura Kakuzo

For hundreds of years, tea farmers have perfected their methods of cultivation for matcha, but demand has begun to increasingly outstrip supply, with domestic stocks of matcha in Japan dwindling due to unprecedented desire for the tea internationally. With climate change also impacting crops and harvests, other countries, such as China and Vietnam, have begun to produce a similar product to keep up with orders in a competitive market. However, due to the strictly protected categorization of matcha, it might be more appropriate to describe these as a 'matcha-like' product, as opposed to a pure matcha itself. While personal tastes and preferences will dictate the types of matcha preferred for incorporating into baking projects or drinks made at home, finding mindful, sustainable ways to consume matcha (that is ethically sourced) will do wonders for keeping a treasured and long-standing tradition and artform alive.

HEALTH

Matcha often elicits a strong emotional response. Some immediately take to the taste; others start off staunchly against it, finding it far too bitter, or are put off by its cloying, powdery texture. Having come this far on the matcha journey, by now you know that these are clearly signs of a beverage that has been inexpertly prepared – a good-quality tea, prepared well, is smooth on the palate. Unlike other things that elicit a similar reaction (say, Marmite), people often persist with trying matcha more than once, due to the purported health benefits that are championed via word of mouth, or on your favourite social media app.

What sets matcha apart from other drinks that are consumed for health benefits is the long history of ritual, tradition, and ceremony, as outlined in previous chapters, which adds a deeper, more holistic dimension to the beverage. Whether you drink it for your mind or your body, it is a tonic that provides a sense of comfort and relief.

BENEFITS FOR THE BODY

Matcha is so much more than just a drink with a pretty, verdant hue. Green tea (*Camellia sinensis*) is regularly consumed across Asia for its numerous health benefits – including antioxidant, anti-inflammatory, and anti-microbial properties – making it a central part of diets around the globe for hundreds of years. Matcha, more specifically, can claim an even wider range of these benefits due to the way it is produced. Unlike *sencha*, or other green teas that are made by infusing tea leaves in water (which are left at the bottom of the cup as dregs, and are not consumed), matcha uses the whole plant, which is ground to a fine powder and emulsified. Because the whole plant is directly consumed, the benefits are more dramatic and potent compared to a tea that might be steeped, where the benefits might be diluted and diffused with the addition of water.

The production process also enhances the health benefits of matcha – growing the tea leaves in the shade, for example, and protecting the plant from direct sunlight allows for a higher level of compounds and amino acids to develop and flourish. The way the leaves are then processed and ground helps to retain some of these more potent benefits, in contrast to the ways other types of tea are traditionally prepared.

Some of the more powerful and active compounds found in matcha include catechins, L-theanine, caffeine, and chlorophyll. Additionally, the selection of vitamins and minerals (more specifically, vitamins A, C, E, and K) are abundant in antioxidant properties. This unique combination has a plethora of cognitive benefits and brings a sense of alertness and focus (without the jitteriness that's often associated with coffee). In addition to promoting the production of beneficial neurotransmitters, stimulating metabolism, and improving focus, matcha is also known for its powerful detoxifying properties. Turns out that strong green colour isn't just for show, after all – it also has some seriously weighty benefits to improve your health, and so it is a worthy option to consider when making healthier lifestyle choices for yourself.

HEALTH BENEFITS

- **For heart health:** Antioxidants present in matcha have been shown to reduce levels of 'bad' LDL cholesterol, improve blood circulation, and help to reduce levels of oxidative stress.

- **For metabolism:** Caffeine and catechins (especially EGCG – Epigallocatechin gallate) work together to increase thermogenesis, or your calorie burning rate, and stimulate fat breakdown, which can enhance exercise by making your workout more effective.

- **For blood pressure:** EGCG can help to lower blood pressure by reducing cholesterol levels and signs of inflammation in the body, as well as improving vasodilation (blood flow).

- **For stress:** The caffeine content of matcha can help to improve focus, while the amino acid L-theanine can promote the production of GABA, a relaxing neurotransmitter. It can also help to regulate cortisol levels in the body.

- **For brain function:** The effect of matcha on long-term cognitive function has been studied extensively and has been shown to be able to protect against a level of cognitive decline in elderly patients, with people reporting better sleep and improved brain function.

- **For skin:** In addition to the antibacterial properties present in catechins, matcha consumption is beneficial for the skin as it is full of vitamins that protect and promote collagen production. The antibacterial properties help to fight acne and rosacea, while the defence brought by matcha can help to reduce hyperpigmentation in the skin, as well as minimize fine lines.

- **For fighting cancer:** Consuming high levels of EGCG has been shown in studies to reduce the size of cancer tumours and inhibit their growth, which can help to supplement any medical cancer treatments as directed by your doctor.

- **For gut health:** The anti-inflammatory properties of matcha have huge benefits for gut health. Not only does matcha provide fibre, it can also aid digestion and promote the growth of good bacteria, as it is a probiotic.

- **For blood sugar:** In its purest form, matcha can help to stabilize blood sugar and improve sensitivity to insulin, however, it is worth noting that any addition of sugar or sweeteners may negate some of the benefits found in the pure tea.

- **For arthritis:** Matcha has been shown to improve bone density and repair, as well as reduce inflammation in the joints, making it a tonic for those suffering with arthritis.

- **For your liver:** Matcha can aid the liver by improving your gut microbiome, and it has been shown to help reduce fat as well as lower inflammation.

- **For detoxification:** Growing matcha in the shade results in a high level of chlorophyll in the plants, which helps to detoxify the body and oxygenate the blood, aiding in the production of red blood cells.

- **For your teeth:** Some of the catechins found in matcha are thought to aid and support dental health, by reducing inflammation of the gums, preventing cavity-causing bacteria, and by helping to strengthen weak tooth enamel. Just like with blood sugar, however, it is important to remember that adding syrups or other sweeteners to your matcha drink will negatively affect your dental care and will not result in the same benefits that a cup of pure matcha offers.

BENEFITS FOR THE MIND

Historically, matcha has played a role in Zen Buddhism, perhaps due to its L-theanine (to promote relaxation) and caffeine (to promote alertness) content, which would have helped to aid lengthy periods of meditation. When visiting a temple in Japan, it is not unusual to be offered a cup of matcha tea (along with some kind of sweet) as refreshment. At Hōkoku-ji temple in Kamakura, for example, visitors are able to enjoy a cup of matcha while admiring a picturesque scene of the bamboo forest that makes up the temple's grounds. For hundreds of years matcha has aided in these moments of mindful contemplation, not just for the drinker, but for the person preparing the matcha, too, as outlined in the heritage chapter on page 21.

Matcha is inextricably tied to ritual. The bamboo *chasen* whisk you might be using to prepare your matcha latte is the same type of instrument that has been used by tea experts and scholars for centuries. The physicality that comes as part of the preparation of matcha – sifting the tea powder, slowly adding the water, and whisking the brush in repetitive motions – requires the type of mental focus that enables us to tap into another, more meditative, state.

Meaningful habits and rituals of this kind are often seen to help alleviate forms of anxiety – giving us a sense of control, and providing a feeling of stability and security in an unpredictable world. Rituals and habits have the power to make mundane, everyday tasks take on a contemplative, spiritual, and sacred power, allowing for moments of gratitude and reflection by making space to let these thoughts in.

MAKING SPACE FOR MATCHA AS PART OF A BUSY AND CHAOTIC LIFE

Taeko Suga (*née* Niimi) is a senior executive at a leading advertising and PR firm, as well as a *sado* tea ceremony practitioner at one of the highest levels at the renowned Urasenke School of Tea. She studied Japanese tea ceremony for over 30 years, driven by a desire to find something for herself that was separate from her career and home life (as a mother of two young children).

For her, the time dedicated to its practice allows her to gain a sense of awareness and perspective that goes beyond the tearoom – to feel a sense of engagement with herself and her immediate surroundings, and to experience seasonal changes and life changes, all of which come into sharp focus as a result of her practice and study of this mindful art.

'In my own hands I hold a bowl of tea; I see all of nature represented in its green colour. Closing my eyes, I find green mountains and pure water within my own heart. Silently sitting alone and drinking tea, I feel these become a part of me.'
– Sen Shoshitsu XV, Urasenke School of Tea

MEDITATION AND MINDFULNESS IN MATCHA PREPARATION

Preparing a delicious cup of matcha is a very subtle alchemy. While deceptively simple, there are a multitude of things that can go awry at any given time – unsifted powder can result in a claggy base, water that is too hot can negatively affect the delicate bouquet of flavours, and over- or under-dilution can make for a disappointing cup of tea. It's necessary to have clarity and focus, and in a traditional *sado* tea ceremony this is a state that practitioners spend years or even decades working towards. In a *chashitsu* (tearoom), every detail is thought out ahead of time, with a great deal of compassion as to how it will be received by guests, and care is taken over how every cup is painstakingly crafted.

While matcha powder of the highest ceremonial grade and quality can take you far, the true art of preparing matcha comes by simply paying attention. This is where the mastery happens, by engaging with the physicality of it – part chemistry, part choreography. With the spirit of the tea ceremony in mind, and following the principles of *wa* ('harmony'), *kei* ('respect'), *sei* ('purity'), and *jaku* ('tranquillity'), when preparing a cup of matcha take inspiration from its long and storied history by taking a chance for a mindful moment – engaging all of your senses, noticing the subtle differences that shift day-to-day, free of distractions.

HERITAGE

'Tea is nought but this; first you heat the water, then you make the tea. Then you drink it properly. That is all you need to know.' – Sen no Rikyū

There is something innately meditative about the process of using matcha as an ingredient. The same tools you might be using to prepare your morning matcha latte (see page 28), like a *chasen* (bamboo tea whisk), *chawan* (tea bowl), and *chashaku* (tea scoop), have been a crucial part of the longstanding Japanese cultural tradition of *chadō* – or the 'way of tea'.

Along with *kado* (the 'way of flowers') and *kōdō* (the 'way of fragrance'), *chadō* (also referred to as *sadō*) is one of the three Japanese Arts of Refinement. Considered study of these artistic practices and rituals invite both the practitioner and the participant to gain a deeper appreciation of the subject from a spiritual, aesthetic, and historical point of view. In the same way a master sommelier, through scent and taste, can impart knowledge about the provenance or terroir of wine, an expert *chajin,* or tea ceremony practitioner, can make keen observations on the way these tools can be wielded to most effectively bring out the flavours and textures of matcha as part of a tea ceremony. The use of bamboo tools, for example, plays an important role in the process, as metal tools can oxidize the tea, causing bitterness. Different bowls are used during summer and winter, due to fluctuations in temperature – and these seasonal changes are reflected by the practitioner in the incense, floral arrangements, and clothing chosen as part of the tea ceremony experience.

THE FOUR GUIDING PRINCIPLES OF THE TEA CEREMONY

WA – 'Harmony'

To find a sense of peace through being in harmony with ourselves, our surroundings, with others, and in nature through compassionate thinking.

SEI – 'Purity'

To approach the ceremony with the purity of space, and the clarity of mind and heart, free from distractions.

KEI – 'Respect'

To have respect for oneself, others, but also for each step of the process.

JAKU – 'Tranquillity'

The ultimate goal – a sense of tranquillity that is gained through the careful application of the previous three principles. A quiet satisfaction in finding balance.

Whether you are a guest at a traditional Japanese tea ceremony or preparing a quick drink for yourself while seeking a moment of quiet contemplation, we can all use the four principles that lie at the heart of the art of *chadō* as a reminder to embrace a sense of mindfulness, gratitude, and appreciation (that can last far longer than the caffeine hit).

Here, we take a look at matcha and its role in Japanese cultural heritage – not only through the principles and philosophies behind this art form, but also the tools

used in this symbolic ritual practice, as well as the significance behind the *chashitsu* tea house.

'The ceremony is a way of worshipping the beautiful and the simple. All one's efforts are concentrated on trying to achieve perfection through the imperfect gestures of daily life.' – Okakuro Kazukō

MATCHA TEA CEREMONY PHILOSOPHY

'*Ichi-go, ichi-e*' is an idiom frequently associated with the Japanese tea ceremony, referencing the ephemeral, unrepeatable nature of an event. The literal meaning of the characters is 'one time, one meeting' and evokes a sense of fleeting beauty, of finding appreciation, gratitude, and comfort within the constant flow of life.

Practitioners of *chanoyū* (the tea ceremony ritual) will spend decades performing a set of proscribed, choreographed routines (referred to as performing *temae*) to capture and tell a story about a specific moment in time, to create and evoke a sense of calm tranquillity for their guests with a cup of carefully crafted tea. Guided by the four core principles of the tea ceremony, and by keeping the spirit of '*ichi-go ichi-e*' in mind, they learn how to host an event with a sense of compassion and with the guests' experience in mind.

The tea ceremony itself is a muted, almost silent affair, but there are messages to be found throughout for those with an observant eye – the calligraphy on display in the tearoom, as well as the *Ikebana* flower arrangement, will often invite the guest to find appreciation in the current season, and subtle changes to the performance will often be made for a variety of reasons. Every movement, every moment, is deliberately arranged for the guests' experience, evoking all the senses: hearing, sight, taste, smell, and touch.

TYPES OF GATHERING

In English, 'Japanese tea ceremony' is used as a catch-all term, but in the art of *chadō*, there are different types of tea-focused events that take place.

Chaji: The more formal in style, *chaji*, or a 'tea event', can take up to four hours. It often includes a *kaiseki* (a multi-course meal), preparing the fire for the ceremony, both *koicha* (thick tea) and *usucha* (thin tea), along with confectionery.

Chakai: Most visitors to Japan will probably have experienced a *chakai* – a 'tea gathering' of around 45 minutes, often with just *usucha* (thin tea) and some confections served in a more informal manner than a *chaji*.

> 'A bath refreshes the body. Tea refreshes the mind.' – Japanese Proverb

MATCHA PREPARATION METHODS FOR THE TEA CEREMONY

While detailed matcha preparation methods can be found on page 48, here we take a look at the symbolic differences between the various ways in which matcha is prepared in the context of a tea ceremony-style event.

Koicha: *Koicha* refers to matcha prepared with a thick, almost syrup-like consistency. It takes an expertly skilled practitioner to get *koicha* right – done improperly, it can be bitter to the point of unpleasantness. Due to its potency, as part of a *chaji* the guests often drink *koicha* from the same tea bowl, and different matcha blends and whisks are used to bring out the properties of the tea so it can be enjoyed in this form. It is almost kneaded, as opposed to whisked, and should be smooth on the palate while being robust and bold in flavour.

Usucha: *Usucha*, or 'thin tea', is perhaps the preparation method most people outside of Japan might be familiar with – it is slightly more approachable, with a characteristic foamy appearance. In a *chaji* or *chakai,* guests would be able to enjoy their own cup of *usucha,* inviting quiet, solitary contemplation.

Chashitsu: The Tea House

Chashitsu tearooms are often purpose-built, in the *sukiya* architectural style, although any room used for the tea ceremony can be referred to as a *chashitsu,* whether freestanding or not. Traditional *shōji* windows, *tatami* bamboo mat floors, and *tokonoma* alcoves for displaying flower arrangements are common features.

Wabi-Sabi Aesthetics and the Tea Ceremony

Sen no Rikyū, in particular, was known for appreciating and incorporating the aesthetic philosophy of *wabi-sabi* as part of the tea ceremony. A muted, rustic visual aesthetic, *wabi-sabi* embraces a quiet, natural beauty – impermanence, imperfection, asymmetry, and finding an appreciation for the transient, fleeting, and ephemeral natural order of things. Prizing simplicity, tea ceremony objects are esteemed for their perceived flaws – the weathered, well-used objects more sought-after than the newer, perfectly preserved objects (see *chawan*, page 28, for the art of *kintsugi*).

CHADŌGU: THE TOOLS

A painter has their paints, a chef might have their knives – and so a tea ceremony practitioner would have their *chadōgu*. Additional details on the tools' usage can be found on page 49.

Chawan: The tea bowl that the guests drink from, arguably the most important part of the tea ceremony. The shape of these might differ depending on the season, with shallower ones in the summer and deeper ones in the winter to cool and retain the temperature of the tea accordingly. Those with slight flaws and imperfections are often admired for their beauty, and examples of repair through *kintsugi* (the art of repairing ceramic with gold) can be found.

Chasen: The bamboo tea whisk used to combine the tea powder and water together. Depending on the type of tea (for example, thick *koicha* versus thin *usucha*) or the different school (such as one of the three *Sen* schools of tea) practices you adhere to, there will be subtle differences based on the treatment of the bamboo and the number of tines of the whisk.

Katakuchi: A spouted serving bowl used to prepare and pour matcha into the *chawan*.

Chashaku: The bamboo tea scoop, used to scoop tea into the *chawan* tea bowl.

Natsume or *usuchaki:* A lacquerware tea caddy used to store matcha for making *usucha* (thin tea).

Cha-ire: The tea caddy or tea container, often made of ceramic for the purpose of storing *koicha* (thick tea).

Kama: The cast-iron kettle used to boil the water for tea.

Hishaku: Often found at temples as well as in tearooms, the *hishaku* is a bamboo scoop used to pour water, often serving a ritual ceremonial role in cleansing before entering temples, as well as within the ceremony.

Mizusashi: A container for cool, fresh water used as part of the ceremony, the *mizusashi* often has aesthetic significance, and it also has an integral role in the ceremony for refilling the *kama* and cleaning the other tools.

Futaoki: A bamboo rest for the head of the *kama* kettle.

Kensui: A bowl for discarded water in the tea ceremony process.

Fukusa: A coloured cloth used to ritually purify the *chadōgu*.

Kusenaoshi: A ceramic holder for the *chasen* whisk, used to dry the *chasen* in its preferred and most desirable shape, also known as a *chasentate* (*chasen* stand).

Chakin: A white cloth, often made of hemp or linen, used to wipe the rim of the *chawan* tea bowl after each guest has taken a sip of their tea.

THE *CHAKAI* CEREMONY: ETIQUETTE

- The ceremonies take place with the hosts and guests sat on their knees on the *tatami* bamboo mat floor.

- The practitioner is essentially curating all elements of the event, so guests are advised to limit any distractions, whether that is wearing perfume, talking during the ritual, or even wearing a watch; all could detract from the atmosphere the host is trying to create.

- While the ceremony should be silent, guests are invited to reflect upon the practice (particularly the *chawan* tea bowl and the flowers) afterwards.

- When the *chawan* is handed to you, it is proper to receive it with your left hand, holding it cupped with both hands. Before drinking, it is customary to turn the bowl 90 degrees clockwise in your right hand before taking a sip. This is not only to best admire the bowl itself, but also to avoid drinking from the same place (in the case of thick *koicha*).

- Sweets or *wagashi* (traditional Japanese confectionery) are offered before the tea is served, to counterbalance some of the tea's bitterness and to leave a rounder finish on the palate.

- The sweet is often eaten in three bites, and the tea is customarily consumed in three sips.

- The ceremony begins before you even step into the room – many *chashitsu* tea houses are surrounded by gardens, and the experience of the guests is curated from this point onwards.

- The practitioner will prepare the tea in front of the guests, but in the spirit of *kei*, or mutual respect, the guests also play a vital role in the ceremony by receiving and showing appreciation. The 'head guest', in particular, plays a significant part in the overall flow of the experience, which can be considered to be a great honour.

'When you hear the splash of the water drops that fall into the bowl you will feel that all the dust of your mind is washed away.' – Sen no Rikyū

Whether as part of an extended ceremony, or a cup of *usucha* served at a shrine or temple, matcha and the ritual behind its preparation and enjoyment are a tangible part of Japan's cultural and historical heritage – what apple pie might be to the Americans or the regional pasta variations may be to the Italians. Innately built into the ritual and preparation of matcha is the space for reflection – how the repetitive movements of whisking matcha might change day by day, month by month, year by year – inviting you to notice the subtle changes along the way.

Matcha and its preparation can serve to bring people together in savouring and appreciation, with perhaps only wine as the other drink that can bring collective groups of people together to admire taste, terroir, and the craftsmanship in a similar way.

Those who dedicate themselves to the study of *chadō* take the core principles of *harmony, respect, purity,* and *tranquillity* to heart not only in the tea house, but aim to apply this in all aspects of their life. Matcha has the power to stay with us once the cup has been drained – its potency and the positive effects from the tea bowl lingering and persisting in a sustained way far beyond.

HISTORY

Matcha as we recognize it today is as emblematic of Japanese culture as high tea might have once been to the English – just as synonymous and as iconic. While this rings true today, the origins of tea prepared in this way come not from Japan, but from China, during the Tang Dynasty (between the 7th and 10th centuries). During this time, tea was often compressed into the form of 'tea bricks' for transportation on the Silk Road trade route, serving as a form of currency, in addition to being a practical way to carry and consume it along the journey.

Powdered tea foamed as part of a ritual gained in popularity during the Song Dynasty (960–1276), used by monks and scholars as part of religious ceremonies. This whisked tea was known as *diancha,* but it fell out of favour in its native China due to the Mongol invasion, as well as the preference for loose-leaf steeped teas during the Ming Dynasty.

The way the tea was historically packaged, steamed, and compressed mirrors the way that matcha is produced and consumed in the modern era, and served as the precursor to matcha in its current form.

WHISKED TEA IN THE KAMAKURA PERIOD

During the Kamakura period (1185–1333), Japan was under the growing rule of the samurai and the upper class, and experiencing a rise in Zen Buddhism. Many of the Zen principles and practices, such as mindful meditation, were adopted and integrated into the samurai's code of conduct (known as *bushido,* or the 'way of the warrior'). The Buddhist priest Eisai is credited with bringing Zen Buddhism to Japan from China, and along with his scriptures he also brought green tea seeds with him after his period of study.

The first seeds were planted by Eisai on Mount Sefuri, on the border of Saga and Fukuoka Prefectures, as well as in Hirado. Matcha tea cultivation grew throughout Japan via his gift of seeds to the monk Myōe (1173–1232) of the Kōzan-ji temple in Kyoto, who planted them in Toganoo and Uji, which remain some of the most renowned producers of matcha today. 'Uji matcha' is in essence the 'Champagne' of powdered green tea – the regional designation a marker of high quality due to its unique cultivation and terroir.

> *'Tea is the most wonderful medicine for nourishing one's health;*
> *it is the secret of long life.'* –Eisai

MYŌAN EISAI (1141-1215)

Eisai was a Buddhist priest and scholar, founder of the Rinzai sect of Japanese Zen Buddhism. After the completion of his studies and certification as a teacher of Zen Buddhism, he returned to Japan from China, and upon his return to Kyushu brought with him tea seeds in addition to his scriptures.

He is widely considered to be one of the 'fathers of Japanese tea', due to his extensive writings on the subject. *Kissa yōjōki* ('drinking tea for health') is considered to be a foundational text that outlined cultivation methods, medicinal benefits, and the use of the tea as a spiritual and religious aid. He is credited with bringing the method of matcha preparation (whisking with a bamboo *chasen*) over from China and first attributing the benefits of matcha consumption to aid meditation for focus.

> *'Tea is the elixir of life.'* – Eisai

KISSA YŌJŌKI

In 1214, Eisai wrote *Kissa yōjōki*, the definitive text at the time on 'drinking tea for health', which exalted the further benefits of tea medicinally (for physical and mental clarity, longevity, and focus), as well as detailing its cultivation, preparation, and serving methods.

According to popular legend, this work spread throughout Japan due to a meeting between Eisai and Minamoto no Sanetomo, the third Shogun of the Kamakura Shogunate. An alcoholic who often suffered from the effects of his drinking the next day, he was prescribed and prepared tea by Eisai, along with a copy of *Kissa yōjōki*. The hangover cure was seemingly incredibly effective and helped to promote the work (and the benefits of tea served and prepared in this way) more widely among the samurai.

MATCHA IN THE MUROMACHI AGE

The term 'matcha' only became part of common parlance during the Muromachi period (1336–1573), as the beverage's role in Japanese society continued to shift from a meditation aid to an aesthetic cultural practice in its own right. Uji, with its proximity to Kyoto, became the de facto matcha capital of Japan, and matcha consumption spread not just from the samurai and ruling classes, but to the masses. Gatherings and events, or *cha yoriai*, began to take place for the proper appreciation of tea, through games and activities like *to cha*, or 'tea fighting', gambling-style games focused on tea tasting. Due to increased trade with China during this period, for the upper classes it was fashionable to enjoy tea while admiring *karamono*, or ornate Chinese tea utensils, ceramics, and artefacts.

The lavish and ostentatious gatherings that took place during this period reflected the *basara* aesthetic of the 14th century, fuelled by trade – a period of flamboyant excess. Tearooms of this time were much larger, the gatherings perhaps more rambunctious and raucous (with the enjoyment of *tocha* making tea parlours perhaps more akin to a pub than of how we imagine the refined stately European tearooms of that time).

Tastes, however, adapted over time, and these larger, more ornate and ostentatious gatherings and tea ware fell out of favour. The shift moved towards aesthetics that prized simplicity and introspection, which were considered to be more refined. Championed by teachers such as Sen no Rikyū and Murata Jukō, this more modest approach was seen to be more in line with an appreciation for the 'spirit of tea', as shown through the concept of *wabi-sabi*. This concept – an aesthetic philosophy that finds beauty and appreciation in imperfection, impermanence, and decay – can find commonalities with many Zen Buddhist teachings, which in turn aligned with the bushido code of the samurai classes.

Tearooms became smaller, to provide a more intimate feel that promoted introspection – the minimalist, pared-back simplicity allowed for the tea, as well as the calligraphy, *Ikebana* flower arrangements, and the tea ware to capture focus.

In the late 16th century, the tea grown for matcha also began to be cultivated using the methods of shading that we are familiar with today. Up until this point they had been grown in direct sunlight, resulting in the deep green colour that has become so popular.

TEA AS CEREMONY: *WABICHA*, *CHADŌ* AND *CHANOYŪ*

Two men are credited more than any other for codifying and formalizing the appreciation of Japanese tea and tea culture (*wabicha*) into an artform in its own right – *Sen no Rikyū* and *Murata Jukō*. Tea ceremony rituals were more formally choreographed, with a focus on the spiritual aspects. Practitioners work to attain proficiency in *chadō,* or the 'way of tea'. This is also referred to as *chanoyū* ('hot water for tea'), and the act or performance of the ceremony itself is referred to as *temae.*

From the heady, hedonistic gatherings of old, which were perhaps less structured, this evolution resulted in the development of several schools of tea, passing down doctrine. The Japanese tea ceremony is full of considered movements, rules, and structure, all created to highlight and best appreciate the tea itself. Matcha being central to this prized cultural and traditional artform helped it to retain its status and relevancy, where it perhaps might have faded or fallen out of favour. The different schools all trace their origins to Sen no Rikyū, as various branches of his descendants explored their own paths and codified these teachings in turn.

SEN NO RIKYŪ (1522-1591)

Born in Sakai, Osaka, Sen no Rikyū served as tea master to two powerful warlords – Oda Nobunaga, followed by Toyotomi Hideyoshi after Nobunaga's death. As tea master he held a considerable amount of influence, serving as an advisor and confidant. Through his relationship with the latter, he even had the honour of serving tea for Emperor Ōgimachi, an event that would have been almost unheard of at the time.

An aesthete, Rikyū popularized the *wabi-sabi* philosophy, and his preference for local Japanese rustic earthenware, as well as his innovative *chashitsu* (tea house) designs, are still regarded as the leading standard of tea ceremony today. In addition to his extensive contribution to the visual aesthetics in the world of tea, he was a prolific writer of definitive texts on the subject, as well as being a talented poet and *Ikebana* practitioner. Three of the major 'schools of tea' have been founded by his descendants, the students of which continue to keep his legacy alive today through annual ceremonies in his honour.

Having held a close relationship with Toyotomi Hideyoshi for many years, their relationship deteriorated and Sen no Rikyū fell out of favour. Upon Toyotomi's instructions, Rikyū was ordered to commit *seppuku* – ritualistic suicide – which he did at the age of seventy. He is buried in Kyoto at the Jūkoin temple, where each tea school created by his descendants takes turns in holding a memorial service on the 28th of each month.

SAN SENKE - THE THREE 'SEN' HOUSES

Three distinct family schools of tea exist today, all founded in Kyoto by direct descendants of Sen no Rikyū. A fourth school, *Sakaisenke*, had existed historically, however Sen no Rikyū's son (Sen no Dōan) died without any heirs or offspring, and so the school died with him.

The other three schools – Omotesenke, Urasenke, and Mushakōjisenke – were founded by the children of Rikyū's grandson, Sen no Sōtan. The different schools are named after their location relative to the Sen estate – the Urasenke branch from the rear, Omotesenke from the front, and Mushakōjisenke along the neighbouring Mushakōji street.

Urasenke is the largest branch, and while the schools share a common ancestor and founding philosophies, they differ in terms of style and presentation of the ritual itself. Urasenke is famed for its frothy, foamy tea using untreated bamboo *chasens* (tea whisks), while Omotesenke uses smoked bamboo whisks for a less foamy tea. Each house will tend to use their own blends of distinctive tea with subtle variations in flavours and production techniques.

MURATA JUKŌ (1423-1502)

Born in Nara in 1423, Murata Jukō is widely regarded to be a pioneer of the *wabicha* style of Japanese tea ceremony. A Zen Buddhist priest, he was one of the first tea masters to champion a more muted approach to the tea ceremony, that came counter to the lavish and opulent tea parties that were in fashion before his time. He is credited as being one of the first to promote the use of the rustic bamboo tea scoop (*chashaku*) instead of the elegant imported *karamono* Chinese scoops that had previously been on trend. His philosophies and writings on the tea ceremony, particularly a document known as *kokoro no fumi,* 'a letter of the heart', were foundational to the principles of Japanese tea ceremony, focusing on rustic simplicity, muted elegance, compassion, and creating an atmosphere of spiritual reverence as part of the ritual.

One of Jukō's students would teach another well-regarded tea master known as Takeno Jō'ō, who would in turn teach Sen no Rikyū.

While the different schools of matcha continue to champion the legacy of the great tea masters and their philosophies on a cultural level, matcha's ties to its roots in Buddhism made it a staple in Japan, consumed not only at temples at times of worship or celebration, but also for its physical and mental benefits.

As tastes adapted and changed, matcha began to be incorporated as an ingredient in new and innovative ways, including in baked goods and confections, and when paired with milk and other sweeteners in latte form, to appeal to new audiences.

The benefits of matcha continued to spread not only within Japan but further afield, particularly as consumers with an interest in health and lifestyle began to adopt its use. The distinctive colour and numerous benefits for health (which are outlined on pages 14–20) resonated and captured the attention of thousands, particularly through the use of social media, with a notable celebrity endorsement from Gwyneth Paltrow, who is often credited with popularizing matcha and bringing it to a new (mostly Western) audience. A once fairly obscure drink, matcha's popularity has skyrocketed in recent years on a global scale, and the evolution of matcha from a meditation aid to contemporary status symbol continues apace, providing consumers of the tea and its fans with benefits for the mind, soul, and body.

CHOOSING & PREPARING MATCHA

HOW TO FIND YOUR PERFECT MATCHA

If you've ever gone shopping for matcha and ended up leaving the store empty-handed because the choice was too great or too confusing, this guide is for you. It will help you cut through the matcha myths and misunderstandings so you can find the right one.

Matcha labels often include terms like ceremonial grade, premium, supreme, AAA, latte grade, or culinary grade/use. In theory, these tell you how high the quality of the matcha is, but they don't actually mean much. There are no industry standards or regulations that guarantee a matcha labelled ceremonial grade is better than one marked for culinary use. So, ignore those terms and look out for the following points when you're buying matcha.

THE PACKAGING

Matcha is normally sold in either a tin or a resealable bag. Tins typically contain smaller portions, and they're associated with a higher-quality product. Tins are airtight and opaque, protecting the matcha from oxygen and sunlight, which will keep it fresh at room temperature. Keep in mind that when it is sold in small quantities, it's assumed you'll consume it within 2–4 weeks.

You can also find quality matcha sold in pouches. However, if the bag is 50–100g (2–4oz) or more, that normally means it's lower grade and best used in lattes and for baking. If you're buying matcha in a pouch, make sure the packaging doesn't have any transparent windows, and reseal the bag tightly once you've opened it.

THE LOCATION

If the packaging lists the location where the tea was grown, that can be a good sign, and also an indication of the kind of flavours you can expect to find in the matcha.

As mentioned on page 7, there are a few key matcha-producing regions. Uji, a small city located between Kyoto and Nara, is Japan's oldest and most famous tea-producing region. Matcha from Uji is considered the best quality, with a bright, grassy flavour and umami-rich creaminess. Uji has become shorthand for quality, which should mean that Uji or Ujicha on a label guarantees a premium product. However, some tea blenders combine a small amount of Uji matcha with lower-grade teas in order to claim they're Ujicha – so it's not foolproof. Look out for further regional details, like where the tea was grown. Wazuka is where most tea leaves for Uji matcha are grown. Tea estates in Kasagi, Minami Yamashiro, and Ujitawara also supply Uji with *tencha*. If your Uji matcha is surprisingly cheap, be suspicious.

Beyond Kyoto, matcha from Fukuoka is usually sweet and mellow with a nutty, toasted flavour. Kagoshima matcha is known to be bright and clean with a smooth richness and minimal bitterness. Matcha from Nishio is typically soft and creamy with a mild flavour – perfect for matcha newbies.

Try to avoid matchas that include very vague locations on their labels. A matcha labelled something like 'Product of Asia' is deliberately obscuring its origins, and is likely to have been grown in China, Vietnam, or South Korea. You can find good-quality matcha produced outside of Japan, but not by tea companies that hide their location. Opt for teas that are transparent about where they come from.

THE PRODUCER

Historically, matchas were made with a blend of *tencha* leaves sourced from across a region. Tea masters would combine them to create a uniform flavour, and different companies became well known for their particular blends. Some of the most famous companies include Marukyu Koyamaen, Ippodo, and Yamamasa Koyamaen (all based in Kyoto), and also Hoshino Seichaen (based in Fukuoka).

Some of these companies, like Ippodo, have been crafting matcha for hundreds of years. If you like to shop by brand, these are the companies to look out for. Try a few of their matchas until you find the blend you like best.

THE CULTIVAR

Because matchas are traditionally a blend of different tea leaves, the cultivars weren't a regular feature on the label or in the product description. Recently, however, tea companies have started to include the cultivars, and some are producing matchas that are marketed as single estate and single origin, meaning they're made with one specific type of *tencha* harvested from one particular estate. These matchas are taking inspiration from coffee culture to give the impression of exclusivity. Some are great; some not so much. It's how the tea is farmed, milled, and blended that makes the biggest difference.

THE MILLING

Only the highest-quality matchas are 100 per cent stoneground, as it's a slow, labour-intensive process. If your matcha is labelled as stoneground, it is likely to be some of the best.

Industrial mills, like jet or ball mills, speed up the process, but there is some debate as to whether they get the texture right or if the heat damages the tea. However, you shouldn't discount industrial milled matcha, or blends of stoneground and industrial, especially for making lattes and smoothies, and for cooking. You don't need expensive, stoneground matcha for a strawberry matcha latte.

THE HARVEST

Matcha is a fresh product, like tea or olive oil, and it goes stale, so the sooner you consume it after harvesting and blending, the better. Labels that include the harvest date, packing date, and a best-before date can help you pick a matcha at its peak flavour.

THE TEA ITSELF

You can't see this in the shop, but when you get your matcha home there are a few signs that your matcha is fresh, good-quality, and going to taste good.

The first is colour. Matcha should be bright green. An electric emerald colour is good. Dull-looking matcha that leans towards khaki or yellow is likely to be stale, or it may have been poorly processed or damaged by heat or light.

When you open your packet or tin of matcha, you should be able to smell it. If your matcha smells grassy, sweet, and vegetal, then it's in peak condition. But if you can't smell much when you open your matcha, or if it smells dusty, fishy, or very bitter, then it's past its best and will not taste great.

Finally, check the texture. It should be fine and silky, like talcum powder. Rub a small pinch of it between two fingers and it should feel soft. Your fingers will slide against each other. But if it feels gritty, it's been coarsely ground, and you'll have trouble trying to whisk it into a creamy-textured drink.

HOW TO STORE MATCHA

Matcha's flavour comes from the aromatic compounds in the tea. These aren't very stable and they degrade over time, or if the matcha is exposed to sunlight, fluctuating temperatures, humidity, and oxygen. Storing your tea correctly will help ensure your first and last matchas taste just as good as each other.

- Keep it out of sunlight – don't be tempted to transfer your matcha to a glass jar to show off its colour. UV-heavy sunlight degrades matcha, bleaching it and causing the matcha to deteriorate. Keep your matcha in an opaque container.

- Keep it airtight – oxygen can also degrade matcha. Most matchas come in an airtight tin or resealable pouch. If it doesn't, invest in a reusable tin that you can decant your matcha into.

- Keep it at a stable temperature – many people suggest storing your matcha in the fridge or freezer, and this is fine for unopened packets of tea. However, once you've opened the tea and started using it, moving it between the fridge and your kitchen (you'll have to bring the tea to room temperature before whisking it) can result in it degrading. It's better to buy matcha in small quantities and store it at room temperature, so you use it up before it has the chance to go stale.

PINK & BLUE MATCHA

You might have seen pink and blue matcha drinks appearing on café menus or in the tea aisle at your local store. These are ground, powdered teas (or, more correctly, tisanes, as they're not made from tea leaves) – but they are not matcha.

Blue matcha is made from the petals of the butterfly pea flower. It's an incredible, vibrant blue colour, rich in antioxidants and caffeine-free. It has a delicate, earthy, floral flavour and is said to be good for relaxation.

CHOOSING & PREPARING MATCHA

Pink matcha is made from dried, ground dragon fruit. It's naturally hot pink in colour and has a sweet, fruity flavour that tastes like a mix of strawberries, kiwi, and melon. It is full of vitamins and minerals, and fans claim that it is anti-inflammatory.

While butterfly pea flower powder and dragon fruit powder aren't matcha, you can use them in the same way. They both make a great latte – especially layered with a shot of matcha – and can be added to smoothies, chia puddings, pancakes, waffles, and bakes. They are ideal for creating spectacular desserts and cakes. *Just don't call them matcha.*

MATCHA LATTE EXTRAS

If you really want to turn your kitchen into a West Coast tea shop, customize your matcha latte with different flavours and add-ins to get that fancy coffee shop at home feel.

The easiest way to add flavour is by using syrups, just like you'd add a pump of syrup to your morning coffee. You don't need to add too much; stir in 1 teaspoon at a time until you get the level of sweetness and flavour that you like. Flavours that blend beautifully with matcha include:

Flavour Extras:
Vanilla
Cinnamon
Almond
Raspberry
Blueberry
Yuzu
Cherry blossom
Earl grey
Salted caramel

If you like your drink to do more than taste nice, you can try a functional add-in to give your morning matcha a sense of purpose. From relaxing mushroom powders to sneaky shots of extra protein, there are a lot of functional ingredients that can be blended into a matcha latte. Before adding a functional ingredient, make sure you read the instructions on the packet so that you understand the safe dosage amount, and check for contraindications for any medications you're taking or health conditions that you have. Some add-ins that are popular with matcha include:

Functional Extras:
MCT oil for an energy boost
CBD oil for a sense of calm
Collagen to support skin health
Lion's mane for brain function
Ashwagandha for reducing feelings of stress
Pea protein for added protein

HOW TO MAKE MATCHA

The simplest way to enjoy matcha is by whisking it with water to make a light, foamy tea with an umami-rich flavour. It takes a few minutes and you will need some matcha-making kit, but it's easy to learn how to do it. Once you have mastered it, you can skip the coffee-shop and tea-house queues and spend the time enjoying a matcha made to your personal tastes instead.

EQUIPMENT

The first thing you need to make a cup of matcha is the right equipment. A classic matcha set includes four tools: the *chasen* (tea whisk), *chawan* (tea bowl), *chashaku* (tea scoop), and a sieve (see page 28 for more on their history and meaning).

Chasen
The simple bamboo *chasen* is essential for making matcha, because using an electric whisk or milk frother to make your matcha risks overmixing the tea, making it bitter.

Chawan
While the tea ceremony calls for *chawans*, any bowl can be a *chawan* if you can make tea in it and drink from it. Use a bowl that is around 13cm (5in) in diameter, is high enough to stop tea sloshing over the sides when you're whisking it, smoothly glazed, and comfortable to hold.

Chashaku
The traditional bamboo *chashaku* is small and narrow – equivalent in size to half a teaspoon. You can also use a teaspoon to measure out your matcha. Alternatively, for ultimate precision, use coffee scales to weigh out your matcha by the gram.

Sieve
A small hand-sifter ensures you get the lumps out of your matcha before you start whisking it, helping you achieve a smooth texture.

PREPARING MATCHA

There are two ways to prepare matcha: *usucha*, or 'thin tea', and *koicha*, or 'thick tea'. For everyday drinking – and for making lattes – *usucha* is the kind of matcha you want to make.

Step 1: The Water
The ideal water temperature for making matcha ranges between 70 and 80°C (158 and 176°F), although some matchas are better brewed at even lower temperatures. If you're not sure, aim for 75°C (167°F).

Getting the perfect water temperature is easy if you have an electric kettle that comes with a range of temperature programmes – but most of us don't. Instead, boil your water then pour some into a bowl/jug and pop in a thermometer. When the thermometer hits 80°C (176°F), start preparing your matcha.

Step 2: The Tools

While the water cools, pour around 100ml (3½fl oz) hot water into your *chawan* and place the *chasen* in it. This warms the bowl and helps to soften the whisk's tines, making them less likely to break when you're whisking the tea. Let them sit for 30 seconds to 1 minute, then pour out the water and dry the bowl thoroughly with a cloth.

Step 3: The Tea

The standard recommendation is to use 2g (approx. ½ teaspoon) matcha to make one cup of *usucha* – approximately 1½ heaped scoops using a *chashaku* or 1 heaped teaspoon. But if you weigh out 2g (approx. ½ teaspoon) matcha, you'll see that's quite a lot of tea. Plenty of people will find that amount of matcha is too strong, even in a latte. For a lighter, more delicate drink, try using just 1 scoop of matcha, which is equivalent to a quarter of a teaspoon or 1g.

When you're adding your matcha to the *chawan*, make sure you sift it to get rid of any lumps. This makes it easier to whisk. Finally, use your *chashaku* to even out the tea in the bottom of the bowl before adding water.

Step 4: The Whisking

For a cup of *usucha*, 70ml (2½fl oz) hot water gives a nice texture and dilution. Measure out the water, then pour it into the *chawan*. Pour around the edges of the bowl first to make sure there's no tea stuck to the sides, then pour water into the middle.

Hold the whisk in your dominant hand and the bowl in your other hand. Place the whisk near the bottom of the bowl and gently knead the water and tea together, making sure there are no dry patches of powder left. Then whisk the tea and water together using a zigzag motion for around 45 seconds. A foam should appear on the top. Once you have as much foam as you like, lift the whisk up and whisk close to the surface of the tea to break down the bubbles. When you have a smooth foam, your matcha is ready.

Step 5: The Clean-up

To clean your *chawan*, pour fresh hot water into the bowl, making sure to angle it down the sides to wash off any foam. Swirl the water in the bowl and discard. Pour in some more water, then dip your *chasen* in and flick a few times to rinse off any matcha. Discard the water and leave the whisk and bowl to dry. Wipe the *chashaku* clean with a dry cloth.

RECIPES

Drinks	54
Breakfasts	92
Baking	116
Desserts	156

MATCHA LATTE

PREP: 5–8 MINUTES • COOK: 1–2 MINUTES • SERVES 1

People who like to start their day with a kick have long relied on coffee. It lands with a jolt and for an hour or two, you feel alert and full of energy. But then comes the crash. Every coffee head knows what it's like to suddenly run out of steam and have to reach for their cafetière. If you want to step off the caffeine roller coaster, swap your morning coffee for a matcha latte; 1 teaspoon of matcha has the same amount of caffeine as a single shot of espresso. But it also has L-theanine, an amino acid that is thought to help you feel calm, relaxed, and focused. Combined with other components in the tea, it helps slow down the body's absorption of caffeine, so you get a gentler increase in your system that lasts longer and declines more slowly. Like coffee, matcha also goes really well with milk, so you can still start your day with a latte. This matcha latte is made with thin *usucha*. If you want a stronger, richer flavour, drop the water down to 50ml (2fl oz) and reduce the milk to 150ml (5fl oz). You'll get a more intense, bright-green drink with a silky texture and intensely savoury flavour.

½–1 tsp matcha

70ml (3fl oz) hot water, approximately 75–80°C (165–176°F)

200ml (7fl oz) full-fat milk

Honey, maple syrup, or agave syrup, to taste (optional)

Follow the method for making matcha on page 49, using ½–1 teaspoon matcha (depending on how strong you would like your matcha to be) and the hot water.

Steam the milk using a milk steamer, or warm in a pan, whisking, until it's steaming hot but not boiling.

Slowly pour the warm milk over the prepared matcha, swirling it around the cup to blend the matcha and milk together. Add a sweetener, such as honey, maple syrup, or agave syrup, if liked, and serve.

MATCHA COLD SHAKE

PREP: 10 MINUTES • COOK: NIL • SERVES 4

If you like your matcha iced and don't have a *chawan* and *chasen*, cold-shake it instead. It seems a bit heretical – and it is – but cold-shaking is a really effective way to blend matcha and water together to make a milder, mellower brew. It's important you sift the matcha before you start, to remove any clumps. Then, when you're shaking the matcha, put all your energy into it. Cold water won't dissolve the matcha powder like hot water does, so it is on you to shake the jar or bottle until the tea and water blend together. When a thick layer of pale green foam develops on the top of the matcha, you can stop shaking. Stirring syrups into cold drinks tends to result in them pooling at the bottom of the glass, so I've added a sweetener to the bottle. That way it gets shaken up along with the matcha and you get an even spread of sweetness. You can leave it out if you don't want to sweeten your drink. Or swap the soda water for tonic water to add some balancing sweetness at the end. Frothy and thirst-quenching, this is a refreshing way to serve matcha. Great for warm sunny days, and perfect if you want to easily make matcha for a crowd.

2 tsp matcha, plus extra to serve

300ml (10½fl oz) cold water

2 tbsp agave or maple syrup

Ice cubes

Chilled sparkling water, to top up

Sift the matcha into a bowl to remove any clumps. Spoon it into a large bottle or jar (a funnel will help to get it into a bottle). Don't use too small a jar or bottle – you need to leave room for the foam to develop.

Pour in 300ml (10½fl oz) cold water and the agave or maple syrup. Seal and shake vigorously for 30 seconds to combine the matcha and the water. The matcha will blend with the water and a thick, pale-green foam will form on top.

Fill 4 glasses with ice and pour in the cold matcha. Top up the glasses with chilled sparkling water. Serve straight away, dusted with a little extra matcha. Reusable straws are optional.

STRAWBERRY MATCHA LATTE

PREP: 10 MINUTES • COOK: NIL • SERVES 1

A Strawberry Matcha Latte is a 21st-century icon. The original matcha Instagram superstar, this drink was invented in San Francisco by Boba Guys, a café specializing in tea drinks. A manager had come back from a tour of Japan with a bag full of speciality KitKats to share with the café owners, Bin and Andrew. What started as a session trying all the different flavours turned into a KitKat cocktail party. When they combined a stick of strawberry and a stick of green-tea-flavoured KitKat in one bite, they knew they had a hit. It was an incredible flavour combination – and one that no one else seemed to have tried. They got to experimenting in the café and Strawberry Matcha Lattes appeared on their menus soon afterwards. The rest is Gen Z history. With a layer of jammy strawberry purée on the base, a mid-section of rich, creamy milk, and earthy matcha floating on top, Strawberry Matcha Lattes taste great and look good on camera. You can't ask for more in a drink.

½–1 tsp matcha

70ml (3fl oz) hot water, approximately 75–80°C (165–176°F)

100g (4oz) fresh strawberries

10g (½oz) caster sugar

Ice cubes

250ml (9fl oz) milk, such as full-fat dairy, oat, or soya

Follow the method for making matcha on page 49, using ½–1 teaspoon matcha (depending on how strong you would like your matcha to be) and the hot water. Set aside to cool slightly.

Hull and roughly chop the strawberries. Scoop them into a small bowl and add the sugar. Using a fork, crush the strawberries until you have a chunky purée. Taste and add more sugar, if needed.

Spoon the strawberry purée into the bottom of a tall glass. Add a generous handful of ice cubes. Slowly pour in the milk. It will float above the strawberry layer.

Pour the prepared matcha through a fine-mesh sieve into the glass (this catches the foam, so you just get the smooth, liquid tea). Serve with optional reusable straws.

MANGO MATCHA LATTE

PREP: 10 MINUTES • COOK: NIL • SERVES 1

Mango and matcha might one day topple strawberry and matcha as the ultimate fruit and tea combination. Lush and sweet, mangoes have a tropical juiciness that cuts through the earthier, more intensely vegetal flavours of matcha. It looks gorgeous in the glass, with the golden layer of mango pooling at the bottom and the pale green matcha floating on the top. You can use any milk to make this latte. I used full-fat dairy, but plant-based milks would be just as good – especially coconut- or vanilla-flavoured soya milk. The major benefit to making this type of latte at home is you get to control the amount of added sugar that goes into the drink, and what kind. I used honey to sweeten the mango with a splash of lime juice to sharpen up the flavours. Depending on the season and the variety of mango you use, you may not need any extra sweetener at all. Blend the mango, and lime juice together, taste, and then add honey (or another syrup, like maple or agave) only if you think it needs it.

½–1 tsp matcha

70ml (3fl oz) hot water, approximately 75–80°C (165–176°F)

100g (4oz) fresh or frozen mango, defrosted if frozen

2 tsp fresh lime juice

2 tsp honey, maple or agave syrup (optional)

Ice cubes

200ml (7fl oz) milk, such as full-fat dairy, coconut, or soya

Follow the method for making matcha on page 49, using ½–1 teaspoon matcha (depending on how strong you would like your matcha to be) and the hot water. Set aside to cool slightly.

Peel and chop the mango, if necessary, then scoop it into a blender. Add the lime juice. Seal and blend until you have a smooth mango purée. Taste and add the honey, if you think it needs it. Blend again.

To assemble the latte, spoon the mango purée into the bottom of a tall glass. Fill the glass most of the way to the top with ice cubes. Slowly pour in the milk. It should float above the mango purée.

Pour the prepared matcha through a fine-mesh sieve into the glass (this catches the foam, so you just get the smooth, liquid tea). Serve with optional reusable straws.

PISTACHIO MATCHA LATTE

PREP: 5 MINUTES • COOK: 1–2 MINUTES • SERVES 1

This might be the most 2020s drink in the book. Two of the decade's most sought-after food trends – pistachio and matcha – in one glass. It's a soft, smooth-textured take on a latte with a hint of candied nuts blending into the grassy-green flavours of the matcha. The drink gets its luxurious mouthfeel from the pistachio cream. If you haven't tried pistachio cream before, prepare to become addicted. A pistachio-based alternative to Biscoff spread or Nutella, pistachio cream is sweet, velvety, and very moreish. In Italy it's used to fill breakfast pastries, and it's delicious stirred into hot drinks – like this matcha latte. The cream melts into the warm matcha, giving the drink a thicker texture, as well as adding sweetness and buttery nuttiness. You could make a pistachio matcha latte just by adding a shot of pistachio-flavoured syrup to a latte, but making it with pistachio cream gives it an extra-special richness.

½–1 tsp matcha, plus extra to serve
70ml (3fl oz) hot water, approximately 75–80°C (165–176°F)
1½ tbsp pistachio cream
200ml (7fl oz) milk, such as full-fat dairy, oat, or soya

Follow the method for making matcha on page 49, using ½–1 teaspoon matcha (depending on how strong you would like your matcha to be) and the hot water.

Spoon the pistachio cream into a heatproof glass or cup. Pour the hot matcha into the glass and stir until the pistachio cream has started to melt into the matcha.

Steam the milk using a milk steamer, or warm in a pan, whisking, until it's steaming hot but not boiling.

Gently pour the warm milk over the pistachio matcha. Dust the top with a little extra matcha powder and serve.

DALGONA MATCHA LATTE

PREP: 10 MINUTES • COOK: 1–2 MINUTES • SERVES 1

DRINKS

Some lockdown trends never made it out of 2020, and some just keep going and going and going. Like Dalgona Coffee. Named after a Korean candy, it's made from instant coffee whipped with sugar and water to make an airy foam that sits on top of hot or cold milk. Originally from Macau – and maybe India before that – it was a huge hit on social media during the Covid-19 lockdowns. And where coffee trends lead, matcha often follows. You can't whip up matcha like instant coffee, but you can whisk it into a sweet meringue that sits like a fluffy green cloud on top of a glass of milk. You can use egg whites or aquafaba (the liquid from a tin of chickpeas) to make the meringue, but remember that it's uncooked. If you use egg whites this drink won't be suitable for the elderly, for pregnant people, or people with compromised immune systems. You can serve your Dalgona Matcha with hot or cold milk. I prefer hot milk, so I can stir the matcha meringue into the milk and melt it. But if you'd like to make a cold version, just fill a glass with ice, pour in cold milk, then spoon the meringue on top.

- 30ml (1fl oz) fresh egg whites or aquafaba
- 1 tbsp caster sugar
- ½ tsp matcha
- 150ml (5fl oz) milk, such as full-fat dairy, oat, or soya

Pour the egg whites or aquafaba into a clean, grease-free bowl. Use electric beaters to whisk until thick, white, and glossy. Stiff peaks should form. Slowly whisk in the sugar, a little at a time, until combined.

Sift the matcha into the whipped egg whites or aquafaba. Whisk until combined.

Steam the milk using a milk steamer, or warm in a pan, whisking, until it's steaming hot but not boiling.

Pour the milk into a heatproof glass or cup. Spoon the matcha foam on top of the milk and serve straight away. You can stir the matcha meringue into the milk to subtly sweeten and flavour it, sip the milk through the matcha meringue, or simply scoop the meringue up and eat it, then drink the milk.

BANANA BREAD MATCHA LATTE

PREP: 10 MINUTES • COOK: 5–10 MINUTES • SERVES 2

If you often find yourself with overripe bananas going black in your fruit bowl and can't stand to make another loaf of banana bread, use them to make this cosy matcha latte instead. Thick, creamy, and warming, it's the matcha equivalent of a pumpkin spice latte. Blending the banana into the oat drink with cinnamon and a dash of maple syrup sweetens it and thickens it up. The result is a deliciously spiced milk that smells like freshly baked cake. Add it to matcha and you get a mellow drink that's comforting and soothing. If cottagecore was a drink, it would be this Banana Bread Matcha Latte. Perfect for sipping on chilly days.

- 1 ripe banana, approximately 100g (4oz)
- 400ml (14fl oz) barista-style oat drink
- 1 tbsp maple syrup
- 1 tsp ground cinnamon
- 2 tsp matcha
- 150ml (5fl oz) hot water, approximately 75–80°C (165–176°F)
- Chocolate sauce, to serve

Break the banana into a blender. Pour in the barista-style oat drink and add the maple syrup and cinnamon. Blend until smooth.

Pour the banana oat drink into a pan and warm until steaming hot, whisking often.

Follow the method for making matcha on page 49, using 2 teaspoons matcha and the hot water.

Pour the matcha into two cups or heatproof glasses, then top up with the hot banana oat drink. Drizzle a little chocolate sauce over the top of each drink and serve.

COCONUT MATCHA LATTE

PREP: 5 MINUTES • COOK: 1–2 MINUTES • SERVES 1

Matcha lattes can be made with almost any kind of milk. Full-fat cow's milk is the classic choice, giving a rich flavour and a balanced sweetness. An oat-based plant milk has a creamy texture but a neutral flavour, which makes it a great base for flavoured lattes, while almond drinks are a popular lower-calorie choice. But there's something extra special about a latte made with a coconut drink. There's a natural sweetness to coconut that teams up well with fresh, grassy notes in matcha. It's a light, refreshing combination that doesn't sit too heavily or fill you up. This latte is made with a barista-style coconut drink, which is normally sold in cartons, rather than the tinned coconut milk. You can also make matcha lattes with coconut milk, but because it's so rich, use a 50/50 mix of coconut milk and almond drink to prevent it becoming too heavy.

½–1 tsp matcha, plus extra to serve

70ml (3fl oz) hot water, approximately 75–80°C (165–176°F)

250ml (9fl oz) barista-style coconut drink

1–2 tsp maple syrup (optional)

Follow the method for making matcha on page 49, using ½–1 teaspoon matcha (depending on how strong you would like your matcha to be) and the hot water.

Steam the coconut drink using a milk steamer, or warm in a pan, whisking, until it's steaming hot but not boiling.

Gently pour the warm coconut drink over the prepared matcha. Take a sip and add a spoonful of maple syrup if you think it needs sweetening. Dust with a little extra matcha. Drink straight away.

MATCHA CHAI LATTE

PREP: 5–8 MINUTES + INFUSING • COOK: 5 MINUTES • SERVES 2

DRINKS

The literal translation of this drink's name is 'powdered tea-tea milk', which is not a bad description of a drink that takes two of the world's most famous tea cultures and smashes them together in a glass with European coffee techniques. In India, masala chai is made by double-boiling black tea with milk, sugar, and spices to make a boldly fragrant, creamy cuppa that's sweet and sustaining. Matcha wouldn't survive the brisk treatment that black tea gets in this process – you'd end up with a very bitter drink. So, rather than simmer the tea with the milk, this recipe gently warms the milk and spices together to recreate the flavours of masala chai. Then the spiced milk is steamed and added to freshly whisked matcha. The loamy, grass-and-greens flavour of the matcha adds an earthy note to the aromatic milk, creating a cosy, full-flavoured drink that will warm you up from head to toe. I used a barista-style coconut drink to make this version, but any plant-based milk or dairy milk would work just as well.

- 450ml (16fl oz) barista-style coconut drink
- 1 tbsp maple syrup, plus extra to serve
- 1cm (½in) thick slice of fresh ginger
- 2 cardamom pods
- 6 black peppercorns
- 2 whole cloves
- ½ cinnamon stick
- ½ tsp fennel seeds
- 2 tsp matcha
- 150ml (5fl oz) hot water, approximately 75–80°C (165–176°F)
- Dried edible flowers, to garnish (optional)

Pour the coconut drink into a pan. Add the maple syrup and all the spices. Set the pan on a medium heat and gently bring to a boil. Take off the heat and set aside to infuse for 5–10 minutes.

Follow the method for making matcha on page 49, using 2 teaspoons matcha and the hot water.

Strain the spice-infused coconut drink through a fine-mesh sieve into a jug. Discard the spices. Either pour the coconut drink back into the pan and gently warm, whisking constantly, until foamy, or use a milk steamer or frother to foam it.

Divide the matcha between two heatproof cups or glasses. Pour in the steamed spiced coconut drink. Taste and add more maple syrup, if you think it needs sweetening. Serve straight away, garnished with dried edible flowers, if liked.

WHITE CHOCOLATE & MATCHA HOT CHOCOLATE

PREP: 5 MINUTES • COOK: 5 MINUTES • SERVES 4

While you can pair matcha with all types of chocolate, matcha and white chocolate is an elite-tier combination. By itself, white chocolate can be a bit cloying and sweet. But add matcha and the powdered tea's grassy bitterness and umami-richness soften the chocolate's sweeter edges, adding a savoury note that brings out the layers of flavour in the chocolate. You'll notice how creamy it is. The vanilla will seem more fragrant. And the cocoa butter tastes more floral and honeyed. There are lots of white chocolate and matcha recipes in the baking and desserts chapters of this book, but if you're keen to try out the combination of white chocolate and matcha, make this hot chocolate first. Smooth, indulgent, and a little bit nostalgic, it's the kind of drink I can imagine enjoying in a snug café with fogged-up windows on a crisp, cold day.

- 1 litre (1¾ pints) full-fat milk
- 125g (4½oz) white chocolate
- 1 tbsp maple syrup
- 2 tsp vanilla extract
- 4 tsp matcha
- 300ml (10½fl oz) hot water, approximately 75–80°C (165–176°F)
- Mini marshmallows, to serve

Pour the milk into a pan. Roughly chop the chocolate and add it to the pan with the maple syrup and vanilla extract. Set the pan on a medium heat and warm, whisking frequently, until the chocolate has melted and the milk is steaming hot. Take off the heat.

Follow the method for making matcha on page 49, using 4 teaspoons matcha and the hot water. You may need to make the matcha in two batches. Don't worry about the tea cooling – the hot milk will warm it back up.

Pour the matcha into four heatproof glasses or cups. Pour in the white chocolate milk. Gently stir to combine. Serve topped with mini marshmallows.

MATCHA MILKSHAKE

PREP: 5–8 MINUTES • COOK: NIL • SERVES 2

Matcha, vanilla, and dairy are a well-established trio; between them, they have a balanced mix of leafy bitterness, floral fragrance, and soft, buttery creaminess. You can always rely on a drink made with these three ingredients to taste good. Just like this bright-green milkshake, which combines vanilla ice cream with matcha to make the ultimate thick shake. Although, vanilla isn't the only ice cream flavour that would work well in this milkshake. Chocolate or strawberry ice cream would also be delicious, while mango or raspberry sorbet would add a refreshing tanginess. If you like your milkshakes extra thick, try adding a handful of fruit. Chopped banana, strawberries, or blueberries would give the milkshake an extra layer of flavour and texture (and maybe even make it count towards your five daily portions of fruit and veg).

2 tsp matcha

150ml (5fl oz) hot water, approximately 75–80°C (165–176°F)

1 heaped tbsp honey

300ml (10½fl oz) full-fat milk

350g (12oz) softened vanilla ice cream

Whipped cream, to serve

Follow the method for making matcha on page 49, using 2 teaspoons matcha and the hot water. Stir the honey into the hot matcha to dissolve it.

Pour the matcha into a blender. Add the milk and vanilla ice cream and blend until frothy and combined.

Pour the Matcha Milkshake into two tall glasses. Top with whipped cream. Serve straight away with reusable straws.

MATCHA YOGURT SMOOTHIE

PREP: 5 MINUTES • COOK: NIL • SERVES 1

This quick and easy breakfast (or any time) smoothie is very adaptable. A simple combination of matcha, yogurt, and honey, you can start the customization by picking the type of yogurt you use. Natural yogurt gives a thinner, more drinkable texture. Greek yogurt packs in more protein and makes a thicker drink. If you prefer to eat plant-based, use a non-dairy soya or coconut milk yogurt and swap the honey for maple or agave syrup. Or boost your gut health by using tangy kefir. Whichever yoghurt you choose, they'll make a satisfying and filling drink blended with matcha – use more or less matcha depending on how bold you want the green tea flavours to be. For more fibre and flavour, add in a handful of your favourite fruit. Banana, strawberries, blackberries, blueberries, mango, or pineapple are all great additions to this smoothie.

½–1 tsp matcha

2 tsp honey

150g (5oz) yogurt, such as natural, Greek, or plant-based

2–3 ice cubes

Reusable straw (optional)

Add all the ingredients to a high-speed blender. Blend until smooth and thick.

Pour the smoothie into a glass and serve straight away. Add a reusable straw as an optional extra.

SPINACH, MANGO & MATCHA SMOOTHIE

PREP: 5–10 MINUTES • COOK: NIL • SERVES 1

If you want to add more matcha to your life without investing in a matcha-making set, try adding it to your morning smoothie. You don't need any extra equipment, beyond the blender you use to whizz up fruit and veg to make a breakfast drink. You don't even need to sift it in; just tip the matcha into your blender, then add your smoothie ingredients. The same flavours that go well with matcha in iced lattes work in a smoothie, too. This green smoothie includes mango for its lush sweetness, then pairs it with iron-rich spinach and a spoonful of chia seeds for extra protein and fibre. It has a silky texture and a juicy, sweet-and-savoury flavour.

½–1 tsp matcha
50g (2oz) baby leaf spinach
125g (4½oz) frozen mango
1 tsp chia seeds, plus extra to serve
250ml (9fl oz) almond drink

Spoon ½–1 teaspoon matcha (depending on how strong you'd like the grassy green matcha flavours to be) into a blender. Add the baby leaf spinach, frozen mango, 1 teaspoon chia seeds and the almond drink. Blend until smoothly combined and thick.

Pour the smoothie into a glass and sprinkle with a pinch of chia seeds. Serve straight away.

EXTRA GREEN MATCHA SMOOTHIE

PREP: 5–10 MINUTES • COOK: NIL • SERVES 1

If you thought smoothies couldn't get any greener, let me introduce you to chlorella. A freshwater algae, it gets its deep green colour from a high concentration of chlorophyll – the same pigment that gives matcha its vibrant hue. Chlorella is a complete protein, which means it contains all nine essential amino acids that the human body can't produce. It's also loaded with B vitamins and is a source of iron and vitamin C. It's thought to be an antioxidant and may help improve blood sugar and cholesterol levels, as well as support your immune system. As with any supplement, you should check for any contraindications before adding it to your smoothies. But if you do want to load up your morning smoothie with chlorophyll, try this refreshing green breakfast drink. It's cooling and hydrating, with a touch of tropical sweetness from the pineapple. The matcha and chlorella combined give it a deep, earthy base note.

75g (3oz) cucumber
1 tsp matcha
1 tsp chlorella powder
50g (2oz) baby leaf spinach
125g (4½oz) frozen pineapple chunks
250ml (9fl oz) coconut water

Chop the cucumber into small chunks, then scoop them into a blender.

Spoon the matcha into the blender, then add the chlorella powder, baby leaf spinach, frozen pineapple and coconut water. Blend until smoothly combined and thick.

Pour the smoothie into a glass and serve straight away.

SPARKLING MATCHA LEMONADE

PREP: 5 MINUTES • COOK: NIL • SERVES 1

Tart and tangy, this sparkling lemonade is a great alternative to super-sweet sodas and mocktails. It only has a pinch of matcha added to it, using the powdered tea like seasoning. The matcha's savoury richness counterbalances the sweetness of the syrup and the lemon's sharpness, bringing them all together and softening their flavours so they meld into a smooth, tasty drink. If you would like a stronger, grassier flavour, up the matcha to ½ teaspoon. On the other hand, if you like your lemonade on the more sugary side, use 1½ tablespoons maple or agave syrup to sweeten the drink. Crisp and refreshing, this is a thirst-quenching, tall drink that's great for hot, sunny days. If you're looking for your next pitcher drink for a summer party or barbeque, this pale green lemonade could be it. Just quadruple the ingredients and serve in a jug filled with ice.

Ice cubes, for shaking and serving
¼ tsp matcha
50ml (2fl oz) cold water
50ml (2fl oz) fresh lemon juice
1 tbsp maple or agave syrup
150ml (5fl oz) soda water, chilled
Lemon slices and mint sprigs, to garnish

Half-fill a cocktail shaker or jar with ice. Sprinkle in the matcha. Pour in the cold water, lemon juice, and maple or agave syrup. Seal and shake together vigorously for 30 seconds or so, until well mixed and chilled.

Fill a tall glass with ice and strain in the matcha lemonade mix. Top up the glass with the soda water and gently stir to mix.

Tuck a slice of lemon and a few mint sprigs into the glass. Serve straight away with reusable straws.

EMERALD PALMER

PREP: 10 MINUTES • COOK: NIL • SERVES 2

An Arnold Palmer is a zero-proof cocktail that's made with a half-and-half mix of black tea and still lemonade. It's named after the American golfer, who used to order it after a long day on the links in California. What black tea can do, matcha can do twice as well. If you cold-shake matcha with lemon and lime juice, a dash of syrup, and water, you get a vivid-green cold brew that is delicious lengthened with soda water. The sour citrus brings out the matcha's creamier, nuttier flavours. When you're pouring in the soda water, be careful of the bubbles. The matcha mix will already be frothy and full of air. Pour the soda water in too quickly and it could foam over the top of your glass. It's a very lively drink.

Ice cubes, for shaking and serving
1 tsp matcha
80ml (2½fl oz) cold water
30ml (1fl oz) fresh lemon juice
30ml (1fl oz) fresh lime juice
1–2 tbsp agave syrup
Chilled soda water, to top up
Lime slices and mint sprigs, to garnish

Half-fill a cocktail shaker or jar with ice. Spoon in the matcha. Pour in the cold water, lemon and lime juices, and 1 tablespoon agave syrup. Seal and shake together vigorously for 30 seconds or so, until well combined and chilled.

Crack open the shaker/jar and dip in a reusable straw. Taste the mix and if it seems too sharp for you, add another spoonful of syrup. Then seal and shake again.

Fill two tall glasses with ice. Strain in the matcha mixture. Top up the glasses with chilled soda water. Lightly stir to combine.

Tuck a few lime slices and mint sprigs into each glass and serve.

MATCHA MOJITO

PREP: 5–10 MINUTES • COOK: NIL • SERVES 2

A twist on the classic Cuban cocktail, Matcha Mojitos began appearing on bar menus and in Instagram posts in the early 2010s. It's not clear who first had the idea to perk up a rum-and-lime mojito with green tea, but the combination quickly spread. Part of the reason must be down to how easy it is to make. Combining matcha in cocktails can be tricky because the powder can clump, but mixing it into a mojito solves that problem because you build the drink in the glass. As everything is muddled together, there's no chance of missing out on its verdant, grassy flavours. Plus, you can really pound it into the lime wedges and sugar to make sure every grain is mixed in. This is a light, refreshing, long drink with a bite of earthiness from the matcha. It's not too boozy or too complex. A great beach holiday drink, it's best enjoyed after a relaxing day in the sun.

25 fresh mint leaves
1 lime, sliced into 6 wedges
2 tbsp granulated sugar
1 tsp matcha
Ice cubes
100ml (4fl oz) golden rum
2 tbsp fresh lime juice
Chilled soda water, to top up

Rub the rim of two collins glasses with a mint leaf to lightly coat it with the herb's aromatic oils, then drop 12 fresh leaves into each glass.

Add 2 lime wedges, 1 tablespoon granulated sugar and ½ teaspoon matcha to each glass. Use a muddler, the end of a rolling pin, or a wooden spoon to crush and muddle them together until the lime wedges have released plenty of juice and the sugar has started to dissolve.

Fill the glasses with ice and pour 50ml (2fl oz) golden rum and 1 tablespoon lime juice into each glass. Stir to mix.

Top up each glass with chilled soda water, stir briefly, then drop in the remaining lime wedges and serve.

MATCHA GIN & TONIC

PREP: 5 MINUTES • COOK: NIL • SERVES 1

Sharp, zesty, and with a touch of sweetness that lingers after every sip, this Matcha G&T will convince you that what your gin and tonic has always been missing is matcha. The choice of Hendrick's Gin is very deliberate. You can make this G&T with your favourite gin if you prefer, but Hendrick's famous cucumber and rose flavours are almost made to go with matcha. The cooling combination of vegetable and floral notes are enhanced by the matcha's savouriness. It gives the aromatics in the gin a boost, backing them up with a layer of umami. The agave syrup is optional. I like adding it to soften the alcohol in the gin, but you can leave it out if you like. Fizzy and bracing, and an eyepopping swampy green colour, this is a delicious daytime drink – because of the caffeine. Although, if you drink espresso martinis at night, a Matcha Gin & Tonic should hold no challenges for you.

Ice cubes, for shaking and serving
½ tsp matcha
50ml (2fl oz) Hendrick's Original Gin
25ml (1fl oz) fresh lime juice
2 tsp agave syrup (optional)
150ml (5fl oz) tonic water, chilled
Lime slices and mint sprigs, to garnish

Half-fill a cocktail shaker or jar with ice. Sprinkle in the matcha. Pour in the gin, lime juice, and agave syrup, if using. Seal and shake together vigorously for 30 seconds or so, until well combined and chilled.

Fill a highball glass with ice and strain in the matcha and gin mix. Top up the glass with the chilled tonic water and gently stir to mix.

Tuck a couple of lime slices and mint sprigs into the glass and serve.

VODKA, LIME & GINGER MATCHA SOUR

PREP: 5 MINUTES • COOK: NIL • SERVES 1

Like the Sparkling Matcha Lemonade on page 82, this cocktail uses matcha more as a seasoning to enhance the other flavours in the drink than as an ingredient you'll be able to taste. The matcha's richness gives the crisp, zesty lime and warm ginger some extra heft. It brightens the drink, so you can taste every layer of flavour. Aside from the matcha, the cocktail follows a standard sour formula of 3–2–1. It's 3 parts alcohol, 2 parts sour, and 1 part sweet. Once you know that ratio, you can try mixing up other sours to see what happens when you add matcha to them. Combinations to try include gin, lemon juice, and simple syrup; silver tequila, lime juice, and agave syrup; and whiskey, lemon juice, and honey. Keep the amount of matcha the same and serve them in a chilled martini or coupe glass.

Ice cubes, for shaking and serving
60ml (2½fl oz) vodka
30ml (1fl oz) lime juice
15ml (½fl oz) syrup from a jar of candied ginger
¼ tsp matcha
¼ slice of kiwi, to garnish

Pop a martini glass in the freezer to chill.

Half-fill a cocktail shaker or jar with ice. Pour in the vodka, lime juice, and ginger syrup. Sprinkle in the matcha. Seal and shake together vigorously for 30 seconds or so, until well combined and chilled.

Take the martini glass out of the freezer. Strain the vodka sour mix into the glass. Fix a quarter slice of kiwi on a cocktail pick and rest it in the glass to garnish it. Serve straight away.

MATCHA MORNING PORRIDGE

PREP: 2 MINUTES • COOK: 10–15 MINUTES • SERVES 1

If the ritual of measuring, sifting, and whisking matcha is the mindful way to make your morning tea, then standing and stirring a pan of porridge until it's rich and thick is the breakfast food equivalent. This porridge is made with a generous splash of oat drink because I like the neatness of pairing oats and oat drink, but any plant-based or dairy milk will work. Use a gutsy, culinary-grade matcha in this porridge. A matcha with lots of savoury, soil, and stem flavours is best. It will give you a bold, green tea flavour that will pair beautifully with the creamy oats.

- 50g (2oz) jumbo porridge oats
- 250ml (9fl oz) oat drink
- ½ tsp matcha
- Maple or agave syrup, to taste
- Fresh raspberries and chopped pistachios, to serve

Tip the oats into a small pan. Pour in the oat drink and sprinkle in the matcha. Stir together.

Set the pan over a medium–low heat and slowly bring to a gentle simmer, stirring constantly.

When the porridge has started to simmer, turn the heat down and gently cook, stirring often, for 5–8 minutes or until the oats are smooth, thick, and creamy. If it seems too dry, add a splash more oat milk.

Ladle the porridge into a warm bowl. Taste and add maple or agave syrup, if you think it needs it. Top with a handful of raspberries and chopped pistachios. Serve straight away.

MINI MATCHA PANCAKE CEREAL BOWL

PREP: 10 MINUTES • COOK: 30 MINUTES • SERVES 2–4

One of the earliest food trends to emerge on TikTok during the first lockdown in 2020, mini pancake cereal was a hit with people who suddenly had time to make breakfast at home. They swapped their regular bowl of cornflakes for a heap of tiny, American-style pancakes piled up on a dollop of yogurt and topped with fresh fruit and honey or syrup. It's easy to understand why this took off during a period when people were stuck indoors with time on their hands. Making dozens of tiny pancakes is time-consuming and you need a lot of patience to stand at the griddle and carefully flip one small pancake after another. But it does look cute. These mini pancakes have a cheerful green colour and bright, leafy flavour thanks to the matcha. They're great served on top of thick Greek yogurt and eaten with whatever fruit is in season. This recipe either serves two generously or four modestly – it depends on how many tiny pancakes you think you can eat.

40g (1½oz) butter, plus extra to cook
125g (4½oz) plain flour
1 tsp baking powder
2 tsp matcha
50g (2oz) caster sugar
A pinch of salt
180ml (6fl oz) full-fat milk
1 large egg
1 tsp vanilla extract
Greek yogurt, fresh fruit, and honey, to serve

Melt the butter and set aside to cool.

Sift the flour, baking powder, and matcha into a mixing bowl. Tip in the sugar. Add a pinch of salt and whisk together with a hand whisk.

Pour the milk into a wide jug or bowl. Crack in the egg and add the vanilla extract. Whisk to combine.

Make a well in the centre of the dry ingredients. Pour the milk into the well and use the whisk to slowly combine the dry and wet ingredients together, whisking until you have a smooth, thick batter. Whisk in the melted butter. Set aside to rest for 5–10 minutes.

Lightly grease a heavy-based frying pan or griddle with butter. Set it on a medium–high heat.

Add ½ teaspoon of the batter to the pan to make a little pancake, and repeat to slowly cover the base of the pan with them. Cook for 1–2 minutes until bubbles form on the top of the pancakes and the edges look firm. Flip them over, using a flexible spatula and a teaspoon to turn them. Cook for a further 1 minute until they're cooked through and golden all over. Scoop onto a warm plate and set aside. Regrease the pan and repeat until you have used up all the batter.

To serve, add a few spoonfuls of Greek yogurt to each serving bowl. Top with the pancakes, your favourite fresh fruit, and a drizzle of honey.

MATCHA & COCONUT CHIA PUDDING

PREP: 5 MINUTES + OVERNIGHT CHILLING • COOK: NIL • SERVES 1

Chia puddings are my go-to breakfast during busy weeks. They take just a few minutes to stir together and can then be left in the fridge overnight to thicken and become creamy (they keep for a couple of days in the fridge). I like to stir up a few at a time (they keep for a couple of days), and I make them in jars so I can grab a chia pudding in the morning, tuck it into my bag, and take it to work. Easy and healthy, it's the perfect start to the day. Chia seeds are a good source of plant-based proteins, as well as fibre. If you'd like to up the protein even more, you could stir protein powder into the pudding or top the pudding with chopped nuts and seeds or nut butters, as well as fruit. Strawberries and pistachios, blueberries and walnuts, raspberries and almonds, blackberries, mango, cherries, and pineapple all make good toppings for this breakfast bowl. They complement the matcha's grassy flavours and the lush, tangy taste of the coconut kefir.

- 250ml (9fl oz) coconut kefir
- 2 tbsp chia seeds
- 1 tsp maple syrup
- ½ tsp vanilla extract
- 1 tsp matcha
- Fresh fruit and nuts, to serve (muesli can also be added as an optional extra)

Pour the coconut kefir into a bowl, serving glass, or jar, and add the chia seeds, maple syrup, and vanilla extract. Sprinkle in the matcha. Stir together, then transfer to the fridge and chill overnight.

In the morning, take the chia pudding out of the fridge and gently stir. It should be thick and creamy. If it's too thick, add a splash more coconut kefir to loosen it. Serve straight away, topped with fresh fruit, chopped nuts, and mint sprigs.

BUTTERMILK & MATCHA BREAKFAST WAFFLES

PREP: 15 MINUTES + RESTING • COOK: 50 MINUTES–1 HOUR • SERVES 4–6

Crisp at the edges with soft, fluffy middles, these matcha-flavoured waffles are a great base for a weekend brunch. The matcha gives them a more green, vegetal flavour than a standard buttermilk waffle, although it's balanced by a small amount of sugar. They're not too sweet and they're not completely savoury, either, so you can take them in any direction you like. Pile them up with crispy fried bacon and scrambled eggs, or stack them with strawberries, whipped cream, and a drizzle of honey. The waffles would also be delicious topped with miso fried mushrooms and snipped chives, or loaded with caramelized peaches and vanilla ice cream. And there's always the option to keep it simple: just a pat of melting butter and plenty of maple syrup. The number of waffles this recipe makes will depend on your waffle maker. How many people it serves depends on how lavishly you're topping them and how hungry your waffle eaters are.

50g (2oz) butter, plus extra for greasing
250g (9oz) plain flour
2 tsp baking powder
2 tbsp matcha
3 tbsp caster sugar
A pinch of salt
275ml (10fl oz) buttermilk
4 eggs, separated
1 tsp vanilla extract
Butter and maple syrup, to serve

Melt the butter and set aside to cool.

Sift the flour, baking powder, and matcha into a large mixing bowl. Add the sugar and a pinch of salt. Use a hand whisk to mix the dry ingredients together.

Pour the buttermilk into a separate bowl. Add the egg yolks (keeping the whites for later) and vanilla extract. Whisk well to combine.

Add a ladle of the buttermilk mixture to the dry ingredients and whisk it in to make a thick paste. Slowly whisk in the remaining buttermilk until you have a smooth batter. Whisk in the melted butter. Cover the bowl with a clean tea towel and set aside for 30 minutes to rest.

After 30 minutes, place the egg whites in a clean, grease-free, non-plastic bowl and whisk with electric beaters until they form soft peaks. Fold the egg whites into the batter with a metal spoon or flexible spatula, trying not to knock out too much air.

Set your oven to its lowest temperature and pop a heatproof plate in there. Grease your waffle irons and cook the batter following the manufacturer's instructions, transferring them to the oven to keep warm.

Serve the warm waffles with butter and maple syrup.

Store: The waffles can be frozen for up to 6 months. Defrost overnight, reheat in the oven or microwave for 30 seconds, then crisp up the waffles in a toaster.

MATCHA OVERNIGHT OATS

PREP: 5–10 MINUTES + OVERNIGHT SOAKING • COOK: NIL • SERVES 1

The inventor of overnight oats – Swiss physician Maximilian Bircher-Benner – has my gratitude. His creation has inspired many of my breakfasts over the years, from traditional Swiss-style soaked muesli to these matcha-flavoured breakfast oats. It's the perfect morning meal for someone like me, who likes to prepare ahead because they know the first few hours of the day are always a rush. This version is made with jumbo porridge oats mixed with matcha and tinned coconut milk – the light version, so they don't end up too thick and heavy – with a dash of syrup for sweetness. Pale green with a clean, earthy richness, they are great paired with tart and tangy raspberries. If you make these oats in a 350–400ml (12–14fl oz) jar, you'll have room to top them with fruit and still be able to fit the lid on so you can take them with you, wherever you're going.

125ml (4½fl oz) light coconut milk, plus extra to serve (optional)

½ tsp matcha

50g (2oz) jumbo porridge oats

1 tsp maple or agave syrup

Fresh raspberries, desiccated coconut, and mint sprigs, to serve

Pour the coconut milk into a bowl, glass, or jar. Sprinkle in the matcha. Whisk together until smoothly combined. If you're using a jar, pop the lid on and give it a good shake to combine the matcha and coconut milk.

Add the porridge oats and the maple or agave syrup. Stir well to mix. Pop into the fridge and leave to soak overnight.

In the morning, give the oats a stir. Add a splash more coconut milk if you think it needs it. Top with raspberries, desiccated coconut, and a couple of small mint sprigs to serve.

MATCHA PANCAKE STACKS

PREP: 10 MINUTES + RESTING • COOK: 20–25 MINUTES • SERVES 4

If you want soft, tender-crumbed pancakes that are light and layered with flavour, use buttermilk. Because it's fermented and acidic, the buttermilk combines with the baking powder to make little bubbles of carbon dioxide, which is what gives these pancakes their fluffy texture. If you don't have any buttermilk available, measure out 110ml (4fl oz) regular milk, stir in the juice from 1 lemon, and leave it for 10–15 minutes until it looks curdled and lumpy. Then use that, even though it looks awful. I promise it will make great pancakes – especially if you add a couple of tablespoons of matcha to the batter. Grassy and earthy, these pancakes are delicious paired with sweet, juicy blueberries and a swirl of thick, creamy yogurt.

25g (1oz) butter, plus extra for greasing
150g (5oz) plain flour
1 tsp baking powder
2 tbsp matcha
50g (2oz) caster sugar
A pinch of salt
110ml (4fl oz) buttermilk
2 eggs
Yogurt, blueberries, desiccated coconut, and maple syrup, to serve

Melt the butter and set aside to cool.

Sift the flour, baking powder, and matcha into a large mixing bowl. Add the sugar and a pinch of salt. Use a hand whisk to mix the dry ingredients together.

Pour the buttermilk into a separate bowl. Break in the eggs. Whisk well to combine.

Slowly trickle the buttermilk mixture into the dry ingredients, whisking constantly, until you have a thick, smooth batter. Whisk in the melted butter. Cover the bowl with a clean tea towel and set aside for 30 minutes to rest.

Set your oven to its lowest temperature and pop a heatproof plate in there. Lightly grease a heavy-based frying pan or griddle with butter. Set it on a medium–high heat. Add 4 heaped tablespoons of the batter to the pan to make 4 pancakes (or more, if your pan is big enough).

Fry for 2–3 minutes until bubbles form on the top and the pancakes are set around the edges. Flip them over, using a flexible spatula or a palette knife, and cook for a further 2 minutes. Transfer to the plate and keep warm in the oven. Repeat, regreasing the pan as necessary, until you have used up all your batter. You should have around 16 pancakes.

To serve, stack the pancakes up, top them with yogurt, blueberries, a sprinkling of desiccated coconut, and a drizzle of maple syrup.

MATCHA MORNING MUFFINS

PREP: 10 MINUTES • COOK: 20–25 MINUTES • MAKES 6

Serve these muffins warm from the oven and you'll convince the most hardened matcha sceptic of the joys of powdered green tea. The matcha in the batter gives the muffins a vibrant green colour and a subtle, nutty richness, while combining soya drink with cider vinegar creates a plant-based alternative to buttermilk, which ensure the muffins have a light and fluffy texture with a tender crumb. The muffins are best eaten on the day they are made, but they can also be frozen.

60g (2½oz) coconut oil
200g (7oz) plain flour
1 tsp baking powder
2 tsp matcha
75g (3oz) caster sugar
A pinch of salt
180ml (6fl oz) unsweetened soya drink
2 tsp cider vinegar
1 tsp vanilla extract

Melt the coconut oil and set aside.

Preheat your oven to 180°C/Fan 160°C/350°F/Gas 4. Line a deep muffin tin with 6 muffin cases.

Sift the flour, baking powder, and matcha into a mixing bowl. Add the sugar with a pinch of salt. Whisk together to combine the dry ingredients.

In a separate bowl, whisk together the soya drink and cider vinegar. Let it sit for a few minutes then whisk in the vanilla extract.

Pour the soya drink mixture and the melted coconut oil into the dry ingredients and fold them together with a flexible spatula or hand whisk. Don't overmix them – it's fine for the batter to be a bit lumpy, just as long as there aren't any visible streaks of dry flour.

Divide the batter between the muffin cases, filling them so they're three-quarters full, and bake for 20–25 minutes until the muffins are risen and springy to the touch. A skewer inserted in the middle should come out clean.

Transfer to a wire rack and let them cool for 10–15 minutes before serving.

These muffins are best eaten on the day they're made, but they will keep for up to 3 days in an airtight container. They can also be frozen for up to 6 months. Take a muffin out of the freezer and let it defrost overnight for a ready-to-go breakfast.

MATCHA SMOOTHIE BOWL

PREP: 10–15 MINUTES • COOK: NIL • SERVES 1

Smoothie bowls first became popular in the 2010s, after Instagram launched and brunches with plenty of visual appeal began to grow in popularity. They are very pretty to look at, and very flexible, too. This Smoothie Bowl is green, of course, to go with the matcha. It gets its thick, velvety texture from the frozen banana, courgette, and spinach, while the kiwi adds a tart sweetness. When I add kiwis to smoothies I leave the skin on for the extra fibre. It blends in completely so you won't even notice it's there, but you can slice it off if you don't like the idea of eating the skin. Vary the toppings to match the seasons and your tastes. Granola, nut butters, mixed seeds, cacao nibs, dried and fresh fruit are all great options.

1 small frozen banana, approximately 100g (4oz)
125g (4½oz) courgette
1 kiwi
25g (1oz) baby leaf spinach
½–1 tsp matcha
100ml (4fl oz) almond drink, chilled
Berries, sliced kiwi, coconut flakes, mixed seeds, granola, lime slices, and mint sprigs, to serve

Peel the banana (if necessary) and break into the blender. Chop the courgette and add to the blender. Chop the kiwi – no need to peel – and add to the blender. Add the spinach. Sprinkle in ½–1 teaspoon matcha (depending on how strong you'd like it to be) and pour in the almond drink. Blend until smooth and thick. Pour into a serving bowl.

Top the smoothie bowl with a handful of berries, some sliced kiwis, coconut flakes, mixed seeds, granola, a lime slice for squeezing, and a mint sprig to garnish. Serve straight away.

ROASTED ALMOND & MATCHA BUTTER

PREP: 15 MINUTES • COOK: 5–8 MINUTES • MAKES 225G (8OZ)

Making your own nut butter feels like performing a magic trick. Initially, as you pulse the nuts in a food processor, they look gritty and grainy, and you think there's no way they'll ever turn into anything as smooth and lush as a nut butter. Then something in the food processor changes and suddenly you're looking at a glossy, silky, plant-based butter. This matcha-enriched version is made with almonds. I used skinned almonds and roasted them for a few minutes until they're golden and toasted – that oven-baked flavour pairs really well with the mix of umami and leafy green notes in the matcha. You can use almonds with their skins on, if you prefer, but it will end up looking a bit swampy. Other nuts that would work well blended with matcha into a butter include cashews, macadamias, hazelnuts, and pecans.

200g (7oz) whole, skinned almonds
2 tbsp coconut oil
1 tsp vanilla extract
2 tbsp caster sugar
2–3 tsp matcha

Preheat your oven to 180°C/Fan 160°C/350°F/Gas 4. Spread the almonds out on a baking tray. Roast them in the oven for 5–8 minutes until golden brown and they smell aromatic. Shake the pan once or twice while they're cooking, to flip the almonds over.

Let the almonds cool for 5–10 minutes. Tip the almonds into a food processor and switch it on to constant. Blend for a few minutes or until the almonds turn to dust and then start to form clumps.

HOW TO STERILIZE A JAR

To sterilize a glass jar, preheat your oven to 160°C/Fan 140°C/325°F/Gas 3. Wash the jar in hot, soapy water (including the lid), then rinse and place on a baking tray. Slide into the oven and heat for around 15 minutes. Take out of the oven and let it cool. Then spoon in your nut butter and seal.

Leave the processor running and start adding the coconut oil, then the vanilla extract, sugar, and 2 teaspoons of the matcha. Keep the processor running until the almonds form a smooth, creamy spread. Taste and add an extra 1 teaspoon matcha if you'd like a stronger flavour. Blitz again to combine.

Transfer the almond spread to a sterilized jar and seal. The nut butter will keep in the fridge for up to 1 month. Great spread on bread, toast, and crackers, used as a topping for smoothie bowls and chia puddings, or as a dip for vegetable crudités.

MATCHA & COCONUT BLISS BALLS

PREP: 15 MINUTES + SOAKING + CHILLING • COOK: NIL • MAKES 8

If you like to hit the gym first thing in the morning and want something quick and portable to eat before or after you work out, make a batch of these protein-laced bliss balls. Naturally sweetened with Medjool dates, they're ideal for grabbing from the fridge on your way out of the house. Soaking the cashews makes them easier to blend and gives the bliss balls a smoother finish. These are rolled in matcha, so you get a really strong green tea hit as soon as you bite into them. If you want a more subtle flavour, use 1 tsp matcha in the Bliss Balls mix, then roll them in 50–75g (2–3oz) desiccated coconut. All the same flavours in a subtler mix.

60g (2½oz) cashews
60g (2½oz) Medjool dates
20g (¾oz) unflavoured, plant-based protein powder
2½ tsp matcha
15g (½oz) desiccated coconut

Tip the cashews into a large bowl and cover with cold water. Leave to soak for 4–8 hours, or overnight.

When you're ready to make the bliss balls, drain the cashews. Tip them into a food processor. Halve the dates and remove the stones. Tear them into the processor. Blitz a few times to start chopping everything and combining them together.

Add the protein powder, ½ teaspoon matcha, and the desiccated coconut. Blitz together, pausing occasionally to scrape the side of the processor, until you have a thick, smooth paste. It may take a few minutes to come together.

Line a baking tray with baking paper. Sift the remaining 2 teaspoons matcha onto a plate.

Divide the protein ball paste into 8 equal-sized chunks. Roll them, one by one, between the palms of your hands to make balls. Then roll them in the matcha to lightly coat. Transfer to the tray.

Place the tray in the fridge and leave for 2–3 hours to firm up. Transfer to an airtight container. They will keep well in the fridge for up to 2 weeks.

JAPANESE MATCHA SOUFFLÉ PANCAKES

PREP: 15 MINUTES • COOK: 15–20 MINUTES • SERVES 2

Tall, airy, and cloudlike, Japanese soufflé pancakes are an elegant addition to modern brunch menus. In spite of their name, they were actually invented in Hawai'i, in a brunch restaurant called Cream Pot. The majority of the restaurant's customers were Japanese tourists, who were disappointed not to find pancakes on the menu. The chef, Nathan Tran, didn't like pancakes, but he did like French soufflés. So, he combined the whisked egg white technique that makes soufflés so fluffy with a delicate pancake batter. The result was a smash with the tourists, who took the idea back to Japan. They can be tricky to make and there are a few key things you have to do to stop them deflating in the pan. The first is to make sure you whisk the egg whites until they're stiff and fold them into the batter gently, without knocking out too much air. Cook them slowly over a low heat, so they cook all the way through – their thickness means you need patience here. Finally, don't take the lid off the pan too quickly. Treat it like an oven with a sponge cake inside it – open the door (lift the lid) too soon and the cake (pancake) will sink. Served with cream, fruit, red bean paste, and a dusting of matcha, they make an extra-special weekend breakfast.

3 large eggs, separated
25g (1oz) caster sugar
1 tbsp full-fat milk
¼ tsp vanilla extract
20g (¾oz) plain flour
½ tsp baking powder
A few pinches of salt
½ tsp cider vinegar
Rapeseed or sunflower oil, to cook
Whipped cream, strawberries, red bean paste (see box, page 14), and matcha, to serve

Slide 2 egg yolks into a large mixing bowl. Slide 3 large egg whites into a separate, large, clean, grease-free bowl that's ideally not made of plastic. The spare egg yolk can be kept in a sealed tub in the fridge for a few days and added to omelettes or used as egg wash for pastry.

Add the sugar to the egg yolks and whisk with electric beaters until combined. Add the milk and vanilla extract and whisk until bubbles form and it looks like it's increasing in volume. Sift in the flour and baking powder. Add a pinch of salt. Whisk together to make a smooth batter. Set aside. *(continued overleaf)*

Add the cider vinegar and a pinch of salt to the egg whites, then use electric beaters (making sure they have been thoroughly cleaned and dried) to whisk until soft peaks form and they look glossy.

Add one-third of the egg whites to the batter and use a flexible spatula or metal spoon to fold them together so they're smoothly combined. Add another one-third of the egg whites to the batter and gently fold them together, trying not to knock out too much air. Repeat with the final portion of egg whites.

Place a lidded frying pan on a low heat and, when it's warm, lightly grease it with a thin layer of rapeseed or sunflower oil.

Add 4 heaped tablespoons of the batter to make 4 rounds. You want to use up half the batter, so top up the rounds with extra batter if needed. Pop a lid on the pan and cook for 2 minutes until the pancakes are starting to look dry.

Top them with spoonfuls of the remaining batter. Pop the lid back on and cook for 8–10 minutes until the bases are golden brown underneath and they look dry. Resist lifting the lid on the pan to look. Trust your nose – if they start to smell sweet and 'cooked', you can take a peek.

Use a spatula to carefully flip the pancakes over. Pop the lid back on and cook for 2 minutes until set and golden brown underneath.

Transfer the pancakes to warm serving plates. Serve them with freshly whipped cream, sliced strawberries, and a spoonful of sweet red bean paste, then dust with matcha. Serve straight away – the pancakes will slowly deflate once they're out of the pan, so eat them as soon as possible.

RED BEAN PASTE

Also known as red bean jam, red bean paste is made with a mix of adzuki beans and sugar and is a popular dessert ingredient in Japan. It has an earthy flavour with a subtle sweetness that adds richness to desserts. You should be able to find it in your local Japanese or Asian supermarket.

MATCHA, WHITE CHOCOLATE & PISTACHIO COOKIES

PREP: 25 MINUTES • COOK: 12–15 MINUTES • MAKES 14

Soft and chewy, these tender cookies are the perfect emergency bake. They don't take long to mix up and, unlike other cookie recipes in this book, the dough doesn't need chilling. You can simply drop scoops of the matcha-flavoured batter onto a baking tray, pop them in the oven, and then 12 minutes later, you have warm cookies ready to eat. Studded with chunks of white chocolate and roasted pistachios, they're a moreish mix of sweet and savoury, with a little bit of salt.

- 110g (4oz) butter
- 110g (4oz) shelled pistachios, roasted and salted
- 150g (5oz) caster sugar
- 1 large egg
- 200g (7oz) plain flour
- 1 tbsp matcha
- 1 tsp baking powder
- A pinch of salt
- 75g (3oz) white chocolate chips

Preheat your oven to 180°C/Fan 160°C/350°F/Gas 4. Line two large baking trays with baking paper.

Melt the butter and set aside to cool. Roughly chop the pistachios and set aside for later.

Using electric beaters, beat together the cooled, melted butter and the sugar until thick. Crack in the egg and beat in. Sift in the flour, matcha, baking powder, and a pinch of salt. Beat together until you have a stiff dough. Stir in the chopped nuts and chocolate chips, then turn out and lightly knead to make a smooth dough.

Divide the mixture into 14 pieces, roll each into a ball, and pop them on the baking trays, leaving generous gaps between them, as the cookies will spread in the oven. Bake for 12 minutes, or until the cookies have flattened and spread a little, look dry, but haven't picked up too much colour. For a firmer cookie, bake for 15 minutes and let the cookies brown a little.

Let the cookies cool on the baking trays for 5 minutes, then transfer to a wire rack to cool completely. They'll keep for 3–4 days in an airtight tin.

MATCHA LOVE HEARTS

PREP: 20–25 MINUTES + CHILLING • COOK: 10–12 MINUTES • MAKES 16

Crisp and buttery with a crumbly texture that melts in the mouth, these simple heart-shaped shortbread cookies could also melt the heart of your loved one – assuming they're susceptible to baked goods. And matcha. Delicious by themselves, they also make a good dessert biscuit. They also make a good dessert biscuit served with the Matcha Ice Cream (see page 173 for the recipe).

- 125g (4½oz) unsalted butter, room temperature
- 60g (2½oz) icing sugar
- 2 egg yolks
- 200g (7oz) plain flour, plus extra for dusting
- 1 tbsp matcha
- A pinch of salt

Beat together the butter and sifted icing sugar in a mixing bowl with electric beaters until soft and creamy. Beat in the egg yolks, one at a time, until the mixture looks silky. Sift in the flour and matcha, then add a pinch of salt. Use your hands or a wooden spoon to work the ingredients together to make a soft dough. If it's too sticky, add a little more flour until you get the texture you want.

Shape the dough into a flat round and wrap in greaseproof paper. Chill in the fridge for at least 1 hour or overnight.

To bake the shortbread, preheat your oven to 180°C/Fan 160°C/350°F/Gas 4. Line two large baking trays with baking paper. Take the dough out of the fridge and let it warm for 10–15 minutes to soften slightly.

Lightly dust your work surface with flour and roll out the dough so it's 5mm (¼in) thick. Use a heart-shaped cutter to stamp out hearts (or use a different-shaped cutter if you're not feeling romantic). Transfer the cookies to the baking tray, leaving a small gap between them – they shouldn't spread too much in the oven. Bake for 10–12 minutes, or until the edges are just starting to look firm. For a crunchier bake, leave them in the oven until the edges brown.

Remove from the oven and cool for 5 minutes on the trays, then transfer to a wire rack to cool completely.

The Love Hearts will keep for up to 5 days in an airtight tin.

MATCHA & ALMOND AMARETTI

PREP: 20–25 MINUTES • COOK: 25 MINUTES • MAKES 16–18

Traditional Italian amaretti are made with just three ingredients: sugar, ground apricot kernels, and egg whites. Also known as bitter almonds, apricot kernels have a rich, nutty flavour with an astringent bite. They also include a compound that can be poisonous in large quantities, so many home bakers swap for ground sweet almonds and a dash of almond essence for a similar flavour. As matcha has a reputation for bitterness, I thought it could work in amaretti, taking the place of almond essence. Its earthy tartness blends with the almonds and evens out the richer, sweeter notes. With a crisp shell and soft middle, they look elegant and are very satisfying to bite into.

80g (3oz) egg whites
125g (4½oz) caster sugar
200g (7oz) ground almonds
1 tbsp matcha
Icing sugar, to coat

Preheat your oven to 170°C/Fan 150°C/325°F/Gas 3. Line a large baking tray with baking paper.

Pour the egg whites into a large, clean, grease-free mixing bowl (ideally not plastic). Use electric beaters to whisk them until soft peaks form and the beaters leave a trail in the mix. Add 1 tablespoon of the sugar and whisk it into the egg whites to combine. Add the remaining sugar and the ground almonds. Sift in the matcha. Use a flexible spatula to fold all the ingredients together until well combined and stiff.

Dust a small plate with icing sugar. Scoop a heaped teaspoon of mixture out of the amaretti mix and roll into a ball using the palms of your hands. Roll the ball in the icing sugar, then place it on a baking tray. Repeat until you have used up all the mixture, topping up the icing sugar as needed. You should have around 16–18 amaretti.

Lightly press each of the amaretti to flatten them a little. Bake for 25 minutes or until pale golden. Let the amaretti cool on the baking tray for 5 minutes, then transfer to a wire rack to cool completely.

Serve by themselves, or as an after-dinner treat. They will keep for up to 7 days in an airtight tin.

MATCHA LINZER COOKIES

PREP: 45 MINUTES + CHILLING • COOK: 20 MINUTES • MAKES 16–17

In the Austrian city of Linz, they have been making Linzertorten since the 17th century. A spiced almond dough filled with fruit preserves and topped with a lattice of pastry – so you can appreciate the jewel-like colour of the filling – a Linzertorte is what you bake for a special occasion. For more everyday celebrations, make Linzer cookies. They're made with a similar almond dough, but baked until crisp and sandwiched together with jam. Importantly, the top cookie has a 'windowpane' cut out of it, so you can see what's inside. To make this matcha twist on the traditional biscuit, I swapped the jam for an emerald-green matcha and white chocolate ganache. It has a lush, silky texture and the grassy aromas pair with the sweet spice in the cookie dough.

For the Linzer Cookies
250g (9oz) plain flour, plus extra for dusting
50g (2oz) ground almonds
1 tsp ground cinnamon
A pinch of salt
100g (4oz) caster sugar
100g (4oz) butter, room temperature
1 large egg
Icing sugar, for dusting

For the Matcha and White Chocolate Ganache
50ml (2fl oz) double cream
50g (2oz) white chocolate
15g (½oz) butter
2 tsp matcha

To make the dough, sift the flour into a mixing bowl, then add the ground almonds, cinnamon, and a pinch of salt. Use a hand whisk to mix then, then set aside.

Tip the sugar into a separate mixing bowl. Add the butter. Use electric beaters to beat them together until soft and fluffy. Crack in the egg and beat until combined.

Add the dry ingredients to the wet ingredients. Gently beat together until they form a soft dough. Shape into a flat round, then wrap the dough in greaseproof paper and chill in the fridge for at least 30 minutes or overnight.

To bake the cookies, preheat your oven to 180°C/Fan 160°C/350°F/Gas 4. Line two large baking trays with baking paper.

Lightly dust your work surface with flour and roll out the dough to a 5mm (¼in) thickness. Use a 6cm (2½in) cookie cutter to stamp out 32–34 shapes – they can be round, fluted, or any shape you like. Cut a small shape out of the centre of half of the cookies using a 3cm (1¼in) cookie cutter. This creates a 'window' for the Matcha and White Chocolate Ganache to show through.

Place the whole rounds on the baking trays, leaving a little gap in between. Bake for 10–12 minutes or until the edges are just golden. Cook the cut-out cookies on a separate baking tray for 8–10 minutes, once the main cookies are finished. Remove from the oven and let the cookies cool on the trays for 5 minutes, then transfer to a wire rack to cool completely.

Meanwhile, make the Matcha and White Chocolate Ganache. Pour the double cream into a small pan and warm over a medium heat until it's steaming hot.

Chop the white chocolate and butter into small chunks and pop them in a small, heatproof bowl. Pour the hot cream over them and stir constantly until the chocolate and butter have melted. Sift in the matcha and stir until smoothly combined. Let the ganache cool, then chill in the fridge for 30 minutes to 1 hour to firm up.

When the cookies and ganache have fully cooled, spread about ½ teaspoon of the ganache onto each base. Top with a 'window' cookie and press down gently so the ganache peeks through the centre.

Pop the cookies on a serving plate. Dust them with icing sugar for a snowy finish, taking care not to cover the ganache. Serve straight away. The Linzer Cookies will keep for up to 3 days in an airtight tin.

MATCHA MUG CAKE

PREP: 5 MINUTES • COOK: 2 MINUTES • SERVES 1

When you find yourself in a cake emergency, reach for a mug cake. Quick, fluffy, and easy to make, this plant-based speed bake takes minutes to cook in the microwave. The ½ teaspoon of matcha in the batter is just enough to add a nutty hint of green tea to the sponge. You can add 1–2 teaspoons if you'd like a more vibrant hit of green tea. Or add another complementary flavour to the batter before microwaving it. A spoonful of strawberry or raspberry jam, a chunk of white or dark chocolate, or a dollop of almond butter or tahini would all work well in this simple cake.

- 1 tbsp coconut oil
- 4 tbsp plain flour
- ¼ tsp baking powder
- ½ tsp matcha
- 2 tbsp caster sugar
- A pinch of salt
- 3 tbsp plant-based milk, such as almond, oat, or soya
- ½ tsp vanilla extract

Melt the coconut oil in the microwave and set aside.

Spoon the flour, baking powder, matcha, and sugar into a 200ml (7fl oz) microwave-proof mug or cup and add a pinch of salt. Whisk together to combine.

Pour in the melted coconut oil, plant-based milk, and vanilla extract and whisk well to mix. Make sure there are no dry, lumpy streaks of flour lurking at the bottom of your mug.

Cook for 90 seconds at 800W. The cake should be risen, firm to the touch, and a little spongy. Adjust the cooking time to your microwave, if it's a lower or higher wattage.

When the mug cake is ready, take it out of the microwave and eat straight away.

MATCHA CHRISTMAS TREE SHORTBREAD

PREP: 45 MINUTES + CHILLING • COOK: 10 MINUTES • MAKES 26

If baking cookies is part of your holiday traditions, try adding these buttery Matcha Christmas Tree Shortbreads to your festive spread. Bright green, thanks to the matcha, and infused with a subtle earthiness, they're not as sugary as some of the classic Christmas cookies. Delicately decorated with a few thin lines of glacé icing and silver 'baubles', they have a well-balanced mix of sweet and savoury flavours. I'm sure Santa would appreciate it if you left a few of these shortbreads out for him on Christmas Eve.

- 125g (4½oz) unsalted butter, room temperature
- 200g (7oz) icing sugar
- 2 egg yolks
- 200g (7oz) plain flour, plus extra for dusting
- 2 tbsp matcha
- A pinch of salt

Scoop the butter into a mixing bowl and sift in 60g (2½oz) of the icing sugar. Beat together with electric beaters until soft and creamy. Beat in the egg yolks, one at a time, until the mixture looks silky. Sift in the flour and matcha. Add a pinch of salt. Use your hands or a wooden spoon to work the dry ingredients into the wet ones to make a soft dough. If it's too sticky, add a little more flour until you get the texture you want.

Shape the dough into a flat round and wrap in greaseproof paper. Chill in the fridge for at least 1 hour or overnight.

To bake the cookies, preheat your oven to 180°C/Fan 160°C/350°F/Gas 4. Line two large baking trays with baking paper. Take the dough out of the fridge and let it warm for 10–15 minutes to soften slightly.

Lightly dust your work surface with flour and roll out the dough so it's 5mm (¼in) thick. Use a Christmas-tree-shaped cutter (or any festive cookie cutter) to stamp out cookies. Reroll the trimmings, as necessary. You should get around 26 cookies, depending on the size of your cutter.

Transfer them to the baking trays, leaving a small gap between them – they shouldn't spread too much in the oven. Bake for 10 minutes or until the edges start to look firm.

Remove from the oven and cool for 5 minutes on the trays, then transfer to a wire rack to cool completely.

To decorate them, sift the remaining icing sugar into a bowl and stir in just enough water to make a spoonable icing. Drizzle or pipe the icing over the cookies in lines, adding little round dots of icing to create baubles. Let the cookies sit for 2–3 hours at room temperature to let the icing harden.

The cookies are delicious by themselves, and they make a great festive gift. They will keep for up to 5 days in an airtight tin.

CHOCOLATE & MATCHA COOKIE SANDWICHES

PREP: 30–40 MINUTES + CHILLING • COOK: 40–45 MINUTES • MAKES 22

Normally, matcha is paired with white chocolate, but smooth and mellow cocoa powder can also work well with the green tea's mown-grass and hedgerow aromas. Especially when it's used to make these crisp, fudgy-tasting, vegan-friendly biscuits. They're sandwiched together with a plant-based icing that's blended with matcha. I first tested the recipe with 1 tablespoon of matcha in the icing, which made a bright green, sweet, and creamy filling for the cookies. Adding 2 tablespoons gave a richer, darker filling with gutsier flavours. Adjust the recipe to suit your tastes.

- 250g (9oz) plant-based spread
- 150g (5oz) soft light brown sugar
- 2 tbsp plant-based milk, such as almond, oat, or soya
- 400g (14oz) plain flour, plus extra for dusting
- 25g (1oz) cocoa powder
- A pinch of salt

For the Matcha Filling
- 150g (5oz) plant-based spread
- 225g (8oz) icing sugar
- 1–2 tbsp matcha
- 1 tsp vanilla extract

To make the cookies, beat together the plant-based spread and the sugar in a mixing bowl with electric beaters until they're light and fluffy. Beat in the plant-based milk. Sift the flour and cocoa powder into the bowl. Add a pinch of salt. Beat together until it forms a smooth dough. Scoop the dough out of the bowl and knead into a flat round. Wrap in greaseproof paper and chill in the fridge for at least 30 minutes to overnight.

Preheat your oven to 180°C/Fan 160°C/350°F/Gas 4. Line three large baking trays with baking paper. Take the dough out of the fridge and let it warm for 10–15 minutes to soften slightly.

Dust your work surface with a little flour and roll out the cookie dough until it's 5mm (¼in) thick. Stamp out rounds using a 6cm (2½in) cutter and arrange on the baking trays, leaving a little gap around each one. Reroll the trimmings as necessary. You should have around 44 cookies. Bake for 20 minutes or until the cookies look firm and dry. You will probably need to do this in batches. Let the cookies cool on the tray for 5 minutes, then transfer to a wire rack to cool completely.

To make the filling, scoop the plant-based spread into a bowl. Sift the icing sugar and matcha into a separate bowl. Beat the icing sugar mix into the spread, a little at a time, until it's combined. Beat in the vanilla extract.

Take one cookie and top it with 1 teaspoon of the matcha filling, then top with another cookie and gently press together. Repeat with the rest of the cookies and the filling. You can serve the cookies as soon as they're filled, but they're better after a few hours chilling in the fridge.

They'll keep for up to 5 days in an airtight container.

COCONUT, MATCHA & DARK CHOCOLATE COOKIES

PREP: 15 MINUTES + CHILLING • COOK: 20 MINUTES • MAKES 20

The combination of coconut and chocolate in these chewy little cookies is probably more controversial than the inclusion of matcha. Personally, I've always loved chocolate bars filled with sweet, sticky coconut. Adding a spoonful of umami-rich matcha to the mix just helps bring the flavours together, turning down the sweetness and bringing out the rich, floral notes in the chocolate. Make sure you give these cookies a good squeeze when you shape them, and don't be tempted to bake them for too long – they're fragile and liable to crumble if overbaked. But get it right and you'll end up with bite-sized cookies that have a crisp, crunchy shell and a chewy centre.

- 125ml (4½fl oz) aquafaba, drained from a tin or jar of chickpeas
- 125g (4½oz) caster sugar
- 175g (6oz) desiccated coconut
- 1 tbsp matcha
- 100g (4oz) dark chocolate, 80% cocoa solids

Preheat your oven to 170°C/Fan 150°C/325°F/Gas 3. Line a large baking tray with baking paper.

Pour the aquafaba into a large, clean, grease-free mixing bowl (ideally not plastic). Use electric beaters to whisk until soft peaks form and the beaters leave a trail in the mix. Add 1 tablespoon of the sugar and whisk it into the aquafaba to combine. Add the remaining sugar and the desiccated coconut to the bowl. Sift in the matcha. Use a flexible spatula to fold all the ingredients together until well combined and stiff.

Scoop a heaped teaspoon out of the coconut mixture and squeeze it to bring it together. Carefully toss it back and forth a couple of times between your hands to shape it into a round, roughly the size of a golf ball. Place it on a baking tray. Repeat until you have used up all the mixture. You should have around 20 coconut cookies.

Bake for 20 minutes or until pale golden and starting to flatten out. Let the cookies cool on the baking tray for 5–10 minutes, then transfer to a wire rack to cool completely.

To decorate the cookies, melt the dark chocolate in a heatproof bowl in the microwave (or in a bowl set over a pan of simmering water, but not touching the water). Line a baking tray with fresh baking paper. Dip the flat side of the coconut cookies into the chocolate, then place them on the lined baking tray, chocolate side down. Once they have all been coated, drizzle any remaining chocolate over the top of the cookies. Chill them in the fridge for 2 hours to set the chocolate.

Serve the cookies by themselves or as an after-dinner treat. The cookies will keep for up to 7 days in an airtight tin.

MATCHA MADELEINES

PREP: 25 MINUTES • COOK: 20 MINUTES • MAKES 18

Airy, delicate, and richly flavoured, madeleines prove that sometimes the simplest-looking bakes are the best. These madeleines are enriched with brown butter, which you make by heating the butter until the milk solids separate and caramelize. The toffee richness of the brown butter brings out the more nutty, toasted flavours in the matcha. Madeleines must be eaten fresh from the oven, as they start to turn rubbery after a few hours. To make life easy, make the batter ahead and chill it. The batter will keep for up to 24 hours. If you want to make these to share with friends, wait until everyone has arrived, then quickly spoon the batter into the moulds and bake. Eaten warm, with a matcha latte on the side, these madeleines will quickly become a teatime favourite.

- 80g (3oz) unsalted butter, plus extra for greasing
- 15g (½oz) honey
- 80g (3oz) plain flour, plus extra for dusting
- 2 large eggs
- 1 large egg yolk
- 60g (2½oz) caster sugar
- 1 tbsp matcha
- ½ tsp baking powder

Chop the butter and add it to a small pan. Set over a medium–low heat and warm until the butter melts. Turn the heat up to medium and simmer, stirring constantly, until the foam starts to subside. Keep cooking and stirring, making sure you scrape up the solids from the base, until the butter is a rich amber colour and the milk solids are golden brown. Take off the heat and carefully pour the butter into a bowl, leaving the milk solids behind. Stir the honey into the melted butter. Set aside.

Preheat your oven to 190°C/Fan 170°C/375°F/Gas 5. Generously butter 18 holes in two madeleine tins and dust lightly with flour, tapping out any excess. Set aside.

Crack the whole eggs into a large bowl, then add the egg yolk and sugar. Whisk together using electric beaters for 2–4 minutes until the mixture is pale, thick, and full of air. The mixture should form ribbons when you lift the beaters out of the bowl.

Sift the flour, matcha, and baking powder into a separate bowl, then sift half this mix into the whisked eggs and sugar. Gently fold together using a flexible spatula, being careful not to knock out the air. Sift in the remaining flour mix and fold until just combined.

Take a spoonful of the matcha batter and mix it into the butter–honey mixture to lighten it, then gently fold the butter–honey mix into the main batter until just combined.

Spoon the batter into the prepared moulds. Bake for 8–10 minutes, or until the madeleines are golden around the edges and spring back lightly when touched. Remove from the oven. Use a palette knife to ease the madeleines from their moulds. Cool on a wire rack for a few minutes.

Madeleines are best eaten within 15 minutes of coming out of the oven. They will be stale within hours, so eat them as soon as you can.

MATCHA & CHOC CHIP SCONES

PREP: 20 MINUTES • COOK: 20–25 MINUTES • MAKES 9

I learned how to make soda bread scones at Ballymaloe, a cookery school in Ireland. Being able to make soda bread was a key skill there, and once we had mastered it we used the basic recipe in all kinds of bakes. Scones were high on the list – plain, fruited, or, like these scones, studded with chocolate chips. Matcha hadn't made it into the pantry back then, but I wouldn't be surprised to see it on the school's curriculum now, especially added to sweet bakes. With crunchy tops and soft, fluffy middles, these scones are delicious served warm from the oven.

- 475g (17oz) plain flour, plus extra for dusting
- 1 tsp bicarbonate of soda
- 1 tbsp matcha
- 2 tbsp caster sugar, plus extra to sprinkle
- A generous pinch of salt
- 100g (4oz) milk chocolate chips
- 250ml (9fl oz) buttermilk
- 1 egg
- 1 tsp vanilla extract
- Milk, to glaze

Preheat your oven to 200°C/Fan 180°C/400°F/Gas 6. Lightly dust a large baking tray with flour.

Sift the flour into a large mixing bowl. Sift in the bicarbonate of soda and matcha, then add the sugar and a generous pinch of salt. Whisk together to combine. Add the chocolate chips and stir them through the dry ingredients. Pour the buttermilk into a separate bowl. Crack in the egg and add the vanilla extract. Whisk together to combine.

Pour three-quarters of the buttermilk mixture into the dry ingredients and use your hand to stir it together to make a soft, slightly sticky dough. If it's too dry, add the rest of the buttermilk. If it's too wet, sift in a little more flour.

Dust your work surface with flour and turn out the dough. Pat it into a rectangle approximately 2.5cm (1in) high. Use a knife to cut the dough into 9 roughly equal-sized pieces.

Place the scones on the baking tray and brush the tops with milk to glaze. Sprinkle with a little extra sugar.

Bake for 20–25 minutes, or until golden brown on top, risen, and they feel light when you pick them up off the baking tray. Cool on a wire rack for a few minutes before serving.

The scones are best eaten on the day they're made. Serve them with butter, raspberry jam, or chocolate spread.

The scones can be frozen for up to 3 months. Defrost overnight and warm for a few seconds in the microwave or oven before serving.

MARBLED MATCHA CHEESECAKE BROWNIES

PREP: 25 MINUTES + FREEZING • COOK: 30–40 MINUTES • MAKES 9–12

When it comes to brownies, people either like them cakey or fudgy. Why not bake a brownie recipe that does both? These dark chocolate brownies have a tangy matcha cheesecake ripple running through them, which helps keep them moist. Then they're baked until the edges are dry and cakey, while the middle still has a silky sheen and mousse-like texture. Plunging the tin straight into an ice bath and then freezing them for a few hours stops the brownies cooking further and sets the two textures. Let them defrost for 30 minutes–1 hour and they'll be the perfect texture for slicing into neat squares.

250g (9oz) butter, room temperature, plus extra for greasing
200g (7oz) dark chocolate, 80% cocoa solids
250g (9oz) caster sugar
3 medium eggs
100g (4oz) plain flour
50g (2oz) cocoa powder
A pinch of salt

For the Matcha Cheesecake Swirl
250g (9oz) full-fat cream cheese
50g (2oz) caster sugar
1 egg
2 tbsp matcha
1 tsp vanilla extract

Preheat your oven to 180°C/Fan 160°C/350°F/Gas 4. Grease and line a 20cm (8in) square baking tin with baking paper. Set aside.

Chop the dark chocolate into small chunks, then melt in the microwave – make sure you check the chocolate every 10 seconds, as it can catch and burn easily. Alternatively, pop the chocolate in a heatproof bowl set over, but not touching, a pan of simmering water. Let the chocolate melt, stirring occasionally. Set aside to cool.

Beat the butter and sugar together with electric beaters until light and fluffy. Beat the eggs into the butter one at a time, beating well between each addition. Pour in the melted chocolate and beat to combine. Sift in the flour and cocoa powder with a pinch of salt. Use a flexible spatula to fold them together. Scrape the mixture into the tin and set aside.

For the swirl, scoop the cream cheese into a separate bowl and beat with electric beaters until soft. Add the sugar and beat until well combined. Crack in the egg. Sift in the matcha and add the vanilla, then beat until well mixed.

Pour the cream cheese mixture on top of the brownie mix in the tin, then use a flexible spatula to turn and fold the two mixtures until they're rippled together. Bake for 30–40 minutes, or until the brownies are set around the edges with a little wobble in the middle. Check after 30 minutes, then keep baking if you think it needs longer.

While the brownies bake, add a few handfuls of ice to a roasting tin and pour in a pool of water. As soon as the brownie tin comes out of the oven, pop it into the ice bath to quickly cool the tin and stop the brownies baking.

When cold, pop the brownies into the freezer for 1–2 hours, still in the tin. To serve the brownies, take them out of the freezer, defrost for 30 minutes–1 hour, then slice into 9–12 squares. Carefully lift from the tin and transfer to a serving plate. The brownies will keep for 3–4 days in an airtight container, or you can freeze them for up to 3 months.

EASY MATCHA CUPCAKES

PREP: 30 MINUTES + COOLING AND SETTLING • COOK: 20–25 MINUTES • MAKES 12

If you love the murkier, more vegetal flavours in matcha, these are the cupcakes for you. They have matcha in both the sponge and the icing, so the green tea flavours are front and centre. The seaweed-green sponges have a deep, mown-grass minerality to them, while the lush, pale-green icing is sweet and creamy. Just a few bites each, these cupcakes are a delicious way to dig deep into the bolder side of matcha-flavoured baking.

250ml (9fl oz) soya drink
2 tsp cider vinegar
100ml (4fl oz) coconut oil
1 tsp vanilla extract
150g (5oz) caster sugar
250g (9oz) plain flour
1 tsp bicarbonate of soda
½ tsp baking powder
1 tbsp matcha
A pinch of salt

For the Icing
150g (5oz) plant-based spread
225g (8oz) icing sugar
1 tbsp matcha
1 tsp vanilla extract

Preheat your oven to 180°C/Fan 160°C/350°F/Gas 4. Line a deep muffin tin with 12 cupcake cases. Set aside.

Pour the soya drink into a mixing bowl. Add the cider vinegar and stir to mix. Set aside for 5–10 minutes. Melt the coconut oil, if you need to, and let it cool.

When the coconut oil is cool, pour it and the vanilla extract into the soya drink. Add the sugar. Whisk them with electric beaters until well combined. It may look lumpy and a bit disgusting – this is the soya drink curdling, which is what you want.

Sift the flour into a separate mixing bowl. Sift in the bicarbonate of soda, baking powder, and matcha. Add a pinch of salt. Beat together to mix.

Pour the wet ingredients into the dry and whisk them together until just combined – don't overmix them, as this will make the cupcakes heavy and dense. Just make sure there are no dry, floury lumps.

Divide the cake batter between the cupcake cases. Bake in the oven for 20–25 minutes, or until the sponges are brown, risen, and springy to the touch. Transfer to a wire rack and let them cool completely.

To make the icing, scoop the plant-based spread into a bowl. Sift the icing sugar and matcha into a separate bowl. Beat the icing sugar, a little at a time, into the spread. Add the vanilla extract and beat together.

Use a palette knife or piping bag to spread the icing over the top of the cupcakes. Let the cupcakes sit for 1–2 hours to set the icing. The cupcakes will keep in an airtight tin for up to 3 days.

MATCHA, WHITE CHOCOLATE & ALMOND BLONDIES

PREP: 20 MINUTES + COOLING • COOK: 45–50 MINUTES • MAKES 9–12

My mum gave these soft, caramelly blondies the ultimate compliment when I tried out the recipe on her: 'not too sweet'. One of the benefits of matcha as an ingredient is its savouriness, which acts as a counterbalance to the sweetness of sugar in cakes and cookies. When you use it in small – or smallish – quantities in baking, you don't necessarily get all the green, vegetal flavours of matcha coming through, but you do get a subtle astringency that dials the sugar down and enhances the other flavours. In these blondies, it's the richness of the nuts and the buttery, floral aromas in the white chocolate.

- 175g (6oz) butter, plus extra for greasing
- 150g (5oz) white chocolate
- 100g (4oz) whole, skinned almonds
- 200g (7oz) caster sugar
- 3 eggs
- 1 tsp vanilla extract
- 175g (6oz) plain flour
- 2 tbsp matcha
- A pinch of salt

Preheat your oven to 180°C/Fan 160°C/350°F/Gas 4. Grease and line a 20cm (8in) square baking tin with baking paper. Set aside.

Chop the chocolate into small chunks and scoop into a large, heatproof mixing bowl. Set aside. Roughly chop the almonds and set aside.

Chop the butter, then pop it in a small pan. Set over a medium–low heat and warm until the butter melts. Turn the heat up to medium and simmer, stirring constantly, until it starts to foam. Keep cooking and stirring, making sure you scrape up the solids from the base, for approximately 7–8 minutes, or until the butter is amber-coloured, the milk solids are browned, and it smells nutty and rich.

Pour the melted butter and the browned milk solids over the chopped white chocolate. Stir until the chocolate has melted. If necessary, briefly heat in the microwave to finish melting the chocolate.

Add the sugar to the chocolate and beat well with electric beaters until well combined. Set aside to cool for 5 minutes, then crack in the eggs and add the vanilla extract. Beat well to combine. Sift in the flour and matcha. Add a pinch of salt. Beat together until well mixed. Add the chopped almonds and use a flexible spatula or a wooden spoon to fold them into the thick batter.

Scrape the batter into the prepared tin. Bake in the oven for 30–40 minutes, or until the edges are set and the middle has a little shimmer to it when you gently shake the tin. Check after 30 minutes, and keep baking if you think it needs longer.

Take out of the oven and let the blondies cool in the tin. Carefully remove the blondies from the tin and slice into 9–12 pieces. Serve warm or at room temperature.

The blondies will keep in an airtight tin for up to 5 days or frozen for up to 3 months.

STRAWBERRY & BUTTERMILK MATCHA CUPCAKES

PREP: 40 MINUTES • COOK: 20–25 MINUTES • MAKES 12

These strawberry jam-filled cupcakes are strangely nostalgic for me, despite matcha not featuring much in my 1990s childhood. The delicate vanilla sponges with their surprise jammy middles remind me of the bakes that used to be sold on the cake stalls at school fetes, while the stiff, matcha-flavoured buttercream is a reassuringly old-fashioned topping for dainty little cakes. I used 1 tablespoon of matcha in the buttercream – enough to give it a light green hue and to smooth out some of the sweetness – but for a stronger hit of green tea, you could double the matcha.

175g (6oz) butter, room temperature
175g (6oz) caster sugar
175g (6oz) plain flour
1 tsp baking powder
A pinch of salt
2 large eggs
1 tsp vanilla extract
100ml (4fl oz) buttermilk
6 tsp strawberry jam
6 strawberries, halved, to garnish

For the Buttercream Icing
150g (5oz) butter, room temperature
300g (11oz) icing sugar
1–2 tbsp matcha
1 tsp vanilla extract
Milk, to loosen (optional)

Preheat your oven to 180°C/Fan 160°C/350°F/Gas 4. Line a deep muffin tin with 12 cupcake cases. Set aside.

Scoop the butter into a large mixing bowl and add the sugar, then beat together using electric beaters until pale and fluffy. Sift in the flour and baking powder. Add a pinch of salt. Slowly beat together until smoothly combined and you have a thick paste. Crack in the eggs, add the vanilla, and beat together until smoothly combined. Pour in the buttermilk and beat again. You should have a smooth, thick batter.

Half-fill every cupcake case with the batter, then add ½ teaspoon of strawberry jam to each and use the rest of the batter to cover the jam. Bake for 20–25 minutes until golden, risen, and springy to the touch. Let the cupcakes cool in the tin for 5–10 minutes, then transfer to a wire rack to cool completely.

To make the buttercream icing, scoop the butter into a large mixing bowl and beat with electric beaters until creamy. Sift in 100g (4oz) of the icing sugar and gently beat into the butter. Repeat, slowly adding the icing sugar until it's all used up. Sift in the matcha and add the vanilla. Beat to combine. If the icing is too stiff, beat in a little milk to loosen it.

Spoon the buttercream icing into a piping bag and pipe it in swirls on top of the cupcakes. Top each cupcake with a strawberry half to garnish and serve.

The cupcakes will keep for up to 3 days in an airtight tin.

MANGO & MATCHA CUPCAKES

PREP: 30 MINUTES • COOK: 20–25 MINUTES • MAKES 8

A cross between a cupcake and cheesecake, these elegant little sponges are almost too sophisticated to be called cupcakes. The bases are flavoured with vanilla and matcha and made with soft brown sugar to give them a subtle twist of toffee. The tangy mascarpone has just enough icing sugar in it to round off the soft cheese's more acidic edges. Most of the sweetness in this cake comes from the mango coulis and fresh mango. I used a ready-made sweet mango sauce to top these cupcakes, having decided that making the sponges and the icing was enough home cooking for one bake. But if you want to make your own, just blend ripe mango with a little bit of icing sugar and a squeeze of lime juice until you get the texture and flavour that you want.

125g (4½oz) butter, softened
125g (4½oz) soft light brown sugar
125g (4½oz) plain flour
1 tsp baking powder
1 tbsp matcha
A pinch of salt
2 large eggs
1 tsp vanilla extract
Mango coulis, to drizzle
½ ripe mango, diced, to decorate

For the Mascarpone Icing
250g (9oz) mascarpone
4 tbsp icing sugar

Preheat your oven to 180°C/Fan 160°C/350°F/Gas 4. Line a deep muffin tin with 8 cupcake cases. Set aside.

Scoop the butter into a large mixing bowl and add the sugar. Use electric beaters to beat them together until soft and fluffy. Sift in the flour, baking powder, and matcha. Add a pinch of salt. Slowly beat together until smoothly combined.

Crack in the eggs, add the vanilla, and beat together. When you have a smooth, thick batter, divide it between the cupcake cases. Bake for 20–25 minutes, or until risen, springy to the touch, and a skewer inserted in the middle comes out clean. Let the cupcakes cool in the tin for a few minutes, then transfer them to a wire rack to cool completely.

To make the mascarpone icing, scoop the mascarpone into a bowl and slowly beat in the icing sugar, 1 tablespoon at a time, until smoothly combined. Keep the icing in the fridge until you're ready to decorate the cupcakes.

Spoon and swirl the icing over the top of the cooled cupcakes. Drizzle over a little mango coulis and then press a few chunks of mango into the top of each cupcake. Serve straight away.

The decorated cupcakes will keep for 2–3 days in the fridge.

MATCHA & LEMON DRIZZLE CAKE

PREP: 20 MINUTES • COOK: 1 HOUR–1 HOUR 10 MINUTES • SERVES 8–10

I used to belong to a baking club that would meet up once a month to share recipes and eat cakes. The first get-together was themed around 'your favourite bake'. Around 20 people came and seven of them made a lemon drizzle cake – including me. Sweet and sharp, lemon drizzles are a joy to make and eat. This plant-based version has matcha added to it, which doesn't just dye the sponge a deep khaki green, but also gives the cake an earthy base note that makes the lemon taste even brighter. It keeps well and is a great cake to have on standby for unexpected guests (or just for regular cake breaks of your own).

- 3 tbsp milled flaxseed
- 8 tbsp water
- 175g (6oz) plant-based spread, plus extra to grease
- 250g (9oz) caster sugar
- Zest and juice of 1 lemon
- 175g (6oz) plain flour
- 1½ tsp baking powder
- 2 tbsp matcha
- A pinch of salt

Whisk together the milled flaxseed and water in a small pan. Warm gently for 5–10 minutes, whisking frequently, until it forms a sticky goo. Set aside to cool and thicken.

Preheat your oven to 160°C/Fan 140°C/325°F/Gas 3. Lightly grease a 900g (2lb) loaf tin with plant-based spread and line the base and sides with baking paper. Set aside.

Scoop the plant-based spread into a bowl and add 175g (6oz) of the sugar. Beat together with electric beaters until pale and fluffy. Scrape in the flaxseed and finely grate in the zest from the lemon. Beat together until smoothly combined. Sift in the flour, baking powder, and matcha. Add a pinch of salt. Fold the flour into the wet ingredients with a flexible spatula until you have a thick, smooth batter.

Scrape the cake batter into the prepared loaf tin and bake for 50 minutes – 1 hour, or until the sponge is risen, springy to the touch, and well browned. A skewer inserted into the middle of the cake should come out clean.

While the cake cooks, juice the lemon into a small pan. Add the remaining 75g (3oz) sugar. Set the pan on a low heat and gently warm, stirring occasionally, for 3–4 minutes, or until the sugar has dissolved and you have a tangy lemon syrup.

When the cake is ready, take the tin out of the oven and poke a few holes in the top of the cake. Pour the lemon syrup over the cake, then set the tin aside to cool completely. When the cake has cooled, carefully turn out of the tin. Serve in slices.

The cake will keep for up to 7 days in an airtight tin.

MARBLED MATCHA & VANILLA LOAF CAKE

PREP: 20 MINUTES • COOK: 45 MINUTES–1 HOUR • SERVES 8–10

While there are more extravagant cakes out there, nothing feels as theatrical to me as a marble cake. It looks so plain and ordinary on the outside, but when you slice into it, an undulating swirl of colours and flavours is revealed. When you cut into this dense, moist loaf cake you'll find a sweet and buttery vanilla sponge threaded with veins of vibrant green matcha. It's not too sweet and will keep for at least a week in an airtight tin.

- 250g (9oz) butter, room temperature, plus extra for greasing
- 200g (7oz) caster sugar
- 300g (11oz) plain flour (or cake flour for a softer texture, if you can find it)
- 3 large eggs
- 2 tsp vanilla extract
- 2 tsp baking powder
- A pinch of salt
- 2 tbsp matcha
- 1 tbsp full-fat milk

Preheat your oven to 160°C/Fan 140°C/325°F/Gas 3. Lightly grease a 900g (2lb) loaf tin with butter and line the base and sides with baking paper. Set aside.

Chop the butter into a mixing bowl. Add the sugar. Use electric beaters to beat together until pale, light, and fluffy – about 2–3 minutes should do it.

Sift the flour into a separate bowl.

Crack 1 egg into the butter and sugar. Add 1 tablespoon of sifted flour. Use the electric beaters to beat together until smoothly combined. Repeat with the remaining 2 eggs, adding 1 tablespoon of flour each time. Beat in the vanilla extract. Tip the remaining flour into the mixing bowl. Sift in the baking powder and add a pinch of salt. Gently beat together until well mixed and you have a thick, smooth batter.

Scoop a third of the batter out of the bowl and pop it into the bowl you sifted your flour into. Sift the matcha into this bowl. Add the milk and beat until combined. Add spoonfuls of the vanilla batter and matcha batter to your prepared loaf tin, alternating them until you have used up all the batter. Drag a skewer or a chopstick through the batter in the tin to ripple them together.

Bake for 45 minutes–1 hour, or until the cake is risen, dark golden brown, and springy to the touch. A skewer inserted in the middle should come out clean.

Take the cake out of the oven and let it cool in the tin before turning it out. Serve in slices.

The cake will keep for up to 7 days in an airtight tin.

MATCHA & RASPBERRY SWISS ROLL

PREP: 30 MINUTES + COOLING • COOK: 10–12 MINUTES • SERVES 10

A light, airy Swiss roll always looks spectacular. But you can elevate it even further by adding matcha to the mix. The fine, fluffy sponge is a great carrier for the green tea's smooth leaf and stem aromas – especially when paired with a sweet berry jam. Add softly whipped cream and you have a trio of colours and flavours that is guaranteed to wow. Don't be afraid of rolling the sponge when it comes out of the oven. Work quickly, while the cake is still warm, and you'll find it's very flexible and easy to roll without cracking. Indulgent enough to serve as a dessert, this Swiss roll would also make a stunning centrepiece for a Japanese-inspired afternoon tea.

Butter, for greasing
110g (4oz) plain flour (or cake flour for a softer texture, if you can find it)
1 tsp baking powder
2 tbsp matcha
A pinch of salt
4 large eggs
110g (4oz) caster sugar

For the Filling
300ml (10½oz) double cream
25g (1oz) icing sugar
150g (5oz) raspberry jam

Preheat your oven to 180°C/Fan 160°C/350°F/Gas 4. Lightly grease a 32cm (12½in) x 24cm (9½in) Swiss roll tin and line with baking paper. Set aside.

Sift the flour, baking powder, and matcha into a bowl. Add a pinch of salt and whisk to combine. Set aside.

Crack the eggs into a large mixing bowl, add the sugar, and use electric beaters to beat them together for a couple of minutes until the mix is pale, foamy, and the beaters leave trails in it as you move them.

Add the flour and matcha mixture to the eggs. Using a flexible spatula, make circular motions to lift and fold everything together, making sure they're well mixed and no floury lumps are visible. Be careful not to knock too much air out of the mixture as you go.

Scrape the mixture into your Swiss roll tin. Tilt the tin to make sure it is evenly coated with the batter. Bake for 10–12 minutes until the sponge looks firm, golden, and has started to shrink away from the edges of the tin.

While the sponge bakes, lay a clean tea towel on your kitchen counter. Top it with a large sheet of baking paper.

When the sponge is ready, take it out of the oven and immediately turn it out onto the lined tea towel. Gently peel the baking paper away from the base of your sponge. Then, take the short end of the tea towel and gently start to roll up the sponge to make a Swiss roll shape. Leave the sponge to cool completely for 2–3 hours.

When you're ready to fill the Swiss roll, whip the double cream and icing sugar together until softly peaking.

Carefully unroll your Swiss roll. Spread the jam over the sponge, then top with the whipped cream. Gently roll up again. Slice the cake onto a serving plate, and eat on the day it's made.

MATCHA FINANCIERS

PREP: 25 MINUTES + CHILLING • COOK: 25 MINUTES • MAKES 8

A convent of French nuns is said to have created the first recipe for Financiers in the 17th century. The kitchens of the Order of the Visitation of Holy Mary, in Annecy, regularly baked small, round almond cakes that the nuns called 'visitandines'. In the 19th century a Parisian baker called Lasne adapted the recipe, changing the shape so the cakes looked like gold bars, and sold them to the financiers who worked in the nearby Paris Stock Exchange. The customers and the cakes ended up with the same name, and we've been baking Financiers ever since. These little cakes have a crunchy outer shell and a soft, yielding centre. The matcha gives them a murky green colour and adds an earthy richness to the brown butter and ground almonds.

- 110g (4oz) unsalted butter, plus extra for greasing
- 40g (1½oz) plain flour
- 2 tbsp matcha
- 150g (5oz) caster sugar
- 150g (5oz) ground almonds
- A pinch of salt
- 125ml (4½fl oz) egg whites
- 8 whole almonds

Chop the butter and add it to a small pan. Set over a medium–low heat and warm until the butter melts. Turn the heat up to medium and simmer, stirring constantly, until the foam starts to subside. Keep cooking and stirring, making sure you scrape up the solids from the base, until the butter is a rich amber colour and the milk solids are browned. Take off the heat and set aside.

Sift the flour and matcha into a bowl. Add the sugar and ground almonds. Add a pinch of salt and whisk together with a hand whisk. Add the egg whites and whisk everything together until well combined and there are no dry, floury lumps. Slowly trickle in the butter, including the milk solids, whisking it in until you have a thick cake batter. Cover the bowl with a tea towel and chill in the fridge for 2 hours or overnight.

Preheat your oven to 190°C/Fan 170°C/375°F/Gas 5. Lightly grease 8 mini loaf tins with butter and line the bases with baking paper. Place them on a baking tray.

Spoon the chilled batter into the greased tins. Pop a whole almond in the middle of each one. Bake for 15–20 minutes, or until the Financiers are risen, golden, and a little crispy-looking around the edges. Let them cool in the tins for 5 minutes, then run a knife around the edges to loosen them and transfer to a wire rack to cool completely.

The Financiers are delicious served warm. They're best eaten on the day they're made, but they will keep in an airtight tin for up to 3 days.

MATCHA, RASPBERRY & WHITE CHOCOLATE LAYER CAKE

PREP: 30 MINUTES + CHILLING • COOK: 30–35 MINUTES • SERVES 12

When the matcha fanatic in your life has a special occasion to celebrate, this is the cake to bake them. A triple-decker tower of delicate, matcha-laced sponges sandwiched together with an indulgent white chocolate and matcha buttercream and then coated in the icing until everything is a beautiful shade of green, it's the kind of cake that gets a wow. When you bake it, you may think it looks a bit small, but it is so rich that it easily serves 12 people, if not more. Top the cake with fresh raspberries to cut through some of the lusher flavours. And if you really love the combination of matcha and raspberry, add a thin layer of raspberry jam to each sponge before topping with buttercream.

Matcha and Vanilla Sponges

350g (12oz) butter, room temperature, plus extra for greasing

350g (12oz) caster sugar

350g (12oz) plain flour (or cake flour, if you can find it)

2 tsp baking powder

3 tbsp matcha

6 eggs

2 tsp vanilla extract

A pinch of salt

Raspberries, to decorate

White Chocolate and Matcha Buttercream

300g (11oz) white chocolate

300g (11oz) butter, room temperature

300g (11oz) icing sugar

1 tbsp matcha, plus extra to dust

Preheat your oven to 180°C/Fan 160°C/350°F/Gas 4. Lightly grease three 18cm (7in) round sandwich cake tins and line the bases with baking paper.

Scoop the butter into a large mixing bowl. Add the sugar and beat together with electric beaters until pale and fluffy.

Sift the flour, baking powder, and matcha into a separate bowl.

Crack 1 egg into the butter–sugar mix and add 1 tablespoon of the flour–matcha mix. Beat together until combined. Repeat with the remaining eggs, adding 1 tablespoon of flour each time. Finally, add the vanilla extract and a pinch of salt and beat together.

Tip in the remaining flour–matcha mix and use a flexible spatula to combine the wet and dry ingredients. Divide between the three cake tins, levelling the tops, then bake for 20–25 minutes, or until risen and springy to the touch. A skewer inserted into the middle should come out clean. Let the cakes cool in the tins for 5 minutes, then transfer to a wire rack to cool completely.

To make the icing, chop the chocolate and scoop it into a microwave-safe bowl and heat it in the microwave, stirring every 10 seconds, until melted. Alternatively, melt in a heatproof bowl set over a pan of gently simmering water, making sure the base of the bowl does not touch the water. Let the chocolate cool for 5–10 minutes.

Scoop the butter into a large mixing bowl and beat until creamy. Add a little of the white chocolate and beat into the butter. Keep adding the white chocolate, a little at a time, until it's all combined with the butter. Sift in half the icing sugar and beat in. Then sift in the rest of the icing sugar and 1 tablespoon of matcha. Beat in so you have a thick, stiff icing.

Take one cake sponge and, if it has a risen dome, slice that off. Place the sponge, cut side down, on a serving plate or board. Spread with 3–4 tablespoons of the icing to cover the top of the cake. Repeat with the next sponge. Slice the risen dome off the final cake and place that, cut side down, on top of the icing. Chill the stacked cakes in the fridge for 30 minutes.

Take the cake out of the fridge. Use a palette knife to coat the top and sides of the cake with the rest of the icing. Chill the cake for 2–3 hours to set the icing.

To serve, sift a little extra matcha over the top of the cake (this is optional), then pile raspberries up on top. Serve in slices.

The cake will keep for 2 days in an airtight tin.

MATCHA COCONUT PUDDINGS

PREP: 15 MINUTES + CHILLING • COOK: 8–10 MINUTES • SERVES 6

A cross between a jelly and a panna cotta, this plant-based pudding is a moreish combination of coconut and matcha with a meltingly creamy texture. I always use vegetarian gelatine to make puddings like these, so they're suitable for most people's diet. Often a mix of carrageenan and locust bean gum, you should be able to find sachets of vegetarian gelatine in the baking aisle of your local supermarket. You can also use agar agar to set these puddings, or just standard gelatine. Whatever you use, read the packet instructions carefully. Different types and brands of gelling agents set different amounts of liquid. Double-check you're using the right amount to make sure you get a lush, velvety set.

2 x 400ml (14fl oz) tins of full-fat coconut milk
10g (½oz) vegetarian gelatine
50g (2oz) caster sugar
1 tbsp matcha, plus extra to garnish
2 tsp vanilla extract
Mint sprigs, to garnish

Give the tins of coconut milk a good shake, then pour the coconut milk into a large pan. Sprinkle in the gelatine and stir until it has dissolved. Add the sugar. Sift in the matcha. Pour in the vanilla extract.

Set the pan on a medium heat and gently warm, whisking frequently, until it comes to the boil.

Take the pan off the heat and ladle the coconut mixture into 6 x 150ml (5fl oz) heatproof ramekins or serving glasses. Let them cool, then chill in the fridge for at least 1 hour or overnight until set.

Just before serving, lightly dust the puddings with extra matcha and garnish with mint sprigs. Best eaten within 2 days of being made.

MATCHA & WHITE CHOCOLATE MOUSSE

PREP: 20 MINUTES + OVERNIGHT CHILLING • COOK: 1–2 MINUTES • SERVES 4–6

A light, airy, French-style chocolate mousse is one of life's easier-to-achieve luxuries. It is often made with just three ingredients: egg whites, chocolate, and a little sugar. This one has a spoonful of green, grassy matcha sifted into the mix before a generous amount of white chocolate is folded in. To make sure the mousse doesn't lose its bubbly texture, whip the eggs into a thick, stiff meringue and try not to knock too much air out when you stir in the chocolate. As this mousse is made with raw egg whites, it won't be suitable for children, the elderly, pregnant people, or people with compromised immune systems. If you don't want to use raw egg whites, you can swap them for 150ml (5fl oz) aquafaba, the liquid from a tin of chickpeas. Whip it up just like the egg whites and then follow the recipe.

- 150g (5oz) white chocolate
- 150ml (5fl oz) egg whites (or aquafaba)
- 4 tbsp caster sugar
- 1 tbsp matcha
- Sliced strawberries, to serve

Break the white chocolate into chunks and pop into a heatproof bowl. Melt in the microwave, stopping and stirring the chocolate every 10–15 seconds until it's smoothly melted. Alternatively, melt the chocolate in a heatproof bowl set over a pan of gently simmering water, but not touching the water. Set aside and let it cool.

Pour the egg whites (or aquafaba) into a clean, grease-free bowl – ideally non-plastic. Use electric beaters to whisk the egg whites until they're thick and stiff peaks form when you lift the beaters out of the bowl.

Whisk in the caster sugar, 1 tablespoon at a time, making sure it's thoroughly incorporated – the egg whites should be stiff and shiny. Sift the matcha into the egg whites, then whisk to combine.

Add the melted chocolate to the whisked egg whites. Use a flexible spatula to fold them together, trying not to knock too much air out of the whipped egg whites.

Spoon the Matcha & White Chocolate Mousse into individual serving bowls or one large serving bowl. Chill overnight until set. Garnish with sliced strawberries and serve.

MATCHA RICE PUDDING WITH SWEET RED BEAN PASTE

PREP: 5 MINUTES • COOK: 30–35 MINUTES • SERVES 4

There is nothing cosier or more comforting than a warm bowl of rice pudding. It's the dessert I reach for when winter first starts to bite. The puddings I grew up eating were made with pudding rice, which typically comes from Italy, although no one will reveal what the actual variety is. Chalky and short-grained, it swells during cooking and becomes plump and tender. The starch it releases thickens the pudding, giving it that satisfying, mouth-coating texture that makes rice pudding so delicious. Pudding rice is still my go-to for recipes like this matcha-flavoured dessert, but other short-grained varieties like arborio, carnaroli, bomba, or glutinous rice would also work.

400ml (14fl oz) tin of full-fat coconut milk
150ml (5fl oz) soya drink
4 tbsp coconut sugar
1 tbsp matcha
A pinch of salt
100g (4oz) short-grain rice
Sweet red bean paste (see page 114) and coconut flakes, to serve

Pour the coconut milk and soya drink into a large pan. Add the coconut sugar and sift in the matcha. Add a pinch of salt. Use a hand whisk to whisk them together.

Tip the rice into the pan. Pop the pan on a medium–high heat and bring to the boil, stirring frequently with a wooden spoon. When the rice pudding starts to boil, turn the heat down to medium–low and gently simmer for 25–30 minutes, stirring often, until the rice is plump and has absorbed most of the liquid.

Take the rice pudding off the heat. You can serve it warm or cold. To serve, spoon it into serving bowls or glasses, then top with a generous spoonful of sweet red bean paste and a few toasted coconut flakes.

MATCHA CRÈME BRÛLÉES

PREP: 10 MINUTES + OVERNIGHT CHILLING • COOK: 20–25 MINUTES • SERVES 6

I like crème brûlées to have a thick layer of lacey, caramelized sugar on top that I have to whack a couple of times to break. It's very satisfying when the sugar finally gives way and I can dive my spoon down into the thick, smooth custard below. Balancing the heap of sugar on top of the crème brûlée is the matcha that's whisked into the custard. It gives the crème brûlées a pungent note of fresh grass and hedgerows that counters the sweetness of the burnt-sugar topping. The perfect make-ahead dessert for a dinner party, assemble these crème brûlées the day before you want to serve them, then add the sugar and caramelize it just before serving.

600ml (1 pint) single cream
1 tbsp matcha
6 egg yolks
4 tbsp caster sugar
3 tsp cornflour
2 tsp vanilla extract
3 tbsp Demerara sugar

Pour the cream into a pan and sift in the matcha. Gently whisk together with a hand whisk. Set over a low heat and slowly warm, whisking often, until the cream is just steaming hot. Take off the heat.

Slide the egg yolks into a heatproof bowl. Add the caster sugar, cornflour, and vanilla extract. Whisk together with the hand whisk until well combined. Slowly trickle the warm cream into the egg yolks, a little at a time, and whisk constantly until the cream is smoothly combined with the egg yolks. Don't add too much at once – you don't want to accidentally scramble your eggs.

Pour the mixture back into the pan and set it over a low heat. Gently warm, stirring with a wooden spoon or flexible spatula, until the matcha custard has started to thicken and lightly coats the back of the spoon. If you lift the spoon out and can swipe a clean line in the custard coating it, the custard is ready. This should take about 8–12 minutes.

Pour the custard through a heatproof, fine-mesh sieve into a bowl or jug, then pour into individual ramekins or heatproof serving dishes. Let the custards cool, then chill in the fridge overnight.

Just before serving, sprinkle the Demerara sugar over the Matcha Crème Brulées. Use a cook's torch, or slide the crème brûlées under the grill and melt the sugar. Let it cool for a few minutes to harden the sugar, then serve.

MATCHA MOCHI

PREP: 25 MINUTES + COOLING • COOK: 2–3 MINUTES • MAKES 8

Stuffed mochi, like these plump, red bean paste-filled mochi, are known as *daifuku* in Japan. They're a type of *wagashi*, a sweet treat that's often served alongside green tea, like matcha. The mochi's sweetness complements the tea's bitter astringency, providing balance. Bouncy and sticky, the mochi dough is easy to make in the microwave. It will be very hot when it comes out of the microwave, so make sure you let it cool before stretching and wrapping it around spoonfuls of sweet red bean paste.

- 125g (4½oz) glutinous rice flour
- 1 tbsp matcha
- 40g (1½oz) caster sugar
- 150ml (5fl oz) cold water
- Cornflour, for dusting
- 8 heaped tsp sweet red bean paste

Sift the flour and matcha into a microwave-safe bowl. Add the sugar and whisk together with a hand whisk. Slowly trickle the water into the bowl, whisking constantly, until you have a smooth batter.

Cover the bowl with cling film and poke in a few holes to let out the steam. Microwave the batter for 1 minute on high (800W). Take out of the microwave and beat well with a wooden spoon. Then re-cover and microwave for a further 1 minute. If the dough is thick and sticky, it's ready. If not, beat again and microwave for 1 more minute.

Lay a sheet of baking paper on your work surface and dust it with cornflour. Turn the dough out onto it and dust the top with cornflour. Let it cool until you can safely handle it.

To make the mochi, divide the dough into 8 pieces. Flatten and stretch one piece into a round approximately 8cm (3in) across. Hold the dough in your non-dominant hand and add 1 heaped teaspoon of red bean paste to the middle. Pinch the dough together over the top of the red bean paste to enclose it. Pop a small cake case on a plate and gently place the mochi in the cake case, seam side down. Repeat with the rest of the dough and red bean paste to make 8 mochi.

You can serve the mochi straight away. They will keep for up to 2 days in an airtight container.

MATCHA & RASPBERRY TIRAMISU

PREP: 30 MINUTES + CHILLING • COOK: NIL • SERVES 6

This famous Italian dessert is normally made with coffee, and is meant to help wake up sleepy diners after they've enjoyed a long lunch. I'm not sure it always works, especially given how much coffee liqueur and Marsala go into the dessert. But I do love Tiramisu, so creating a matcha-flavoured version for this book was a must. The matcha is mixed with raspberry liqueur, to ensure the pudding has a little kick, and paired with fresh raspberries for sharpness. As this dish is made with raw egg whites it won't be suitable for children, the elderly, pregnant people, or people with compromised immune systems, so please keep this in mind when you're serving it.

- 1 tbsp matcha, plus extra for dusting
- 225ml (8fl oz) hot water, approximately 75–80°C (165–176°F)
- 2 eggs
- 3 tbsp caster sugar
- 450g (1lb) mascarpone cheese
- 30ml (1fl oz) marsala wine
- 75ml (3fl oz) raspberry liqueur
- 42 Savoiardi sponge fingers
- Raspberries, to serve

Sift 1 tablespoon of matcha into a heatproof bowl. Add the hot water and whisk until smoothly combined, following the method on page 49. Set aside to cool.

Crack the eggs and separate them into two clean, grease-free bowls, ideally non-plastic. Use electric beaters to whisk the egg whites until stiff peaks form when you lift the beaters from the bowl. Set aside.

Add the sugar to the egg yolks and beat with the electric beaters until they're pale and thick. Beat in the mascarpone, then beat in the marsala. Fold the stiff egg whites into the mascarpone mix using a flexible spatula.

Add the raspberry liqueur to the cooled matcha. Dip one-third of the sponge fingers in the matcha and use them to line the base of 6 x 300ml (10½fl oz) glasses or a large, 2-litre (2¼-pint) dish. You may need to break the sponge fingers in half to line the glasses. Top with one-third of the mascarpone mixture. Dust over enough matcha to lightly coat them.

Repeat with another one-third of the sponge fingers, dipping them in the matcha. Then top with another layer of mascarpone. Dust with matcha. Repeat with the final sponge fingers, matcha dipping, and mascarpone mixture. Dust with a final layer of matcha. Chill in the fridge for at least 12 hours. Tiramisu is best made 24 hours before you want to serve it.

To serve, add a few raspberries to the top of each glass. Best eaten within 2 days of being made.

MATCHA AFFOGATO

PREP: 5 MINUTES • COOK: NIL • SERVES 1

If you can make it with coffee, you can make it better with matcha. Never is that truer than when it comes to affogato. The name means 'drowned' in Italian, and normally the ice cream is sinking under a shot of hot, bitter espresso. For this green tea version, I made a *koicha*-style shot of matcha with 40ml (1½fl oz) hot water. This thicker method of brewing matcha produces a more lustrous drink with a syrupier mouthfeel than the thinner, *usucha*-style of matcha. It has a robust flavour that can take on the ice cream's dairy-rich sweetness. Unlike an espresso affogato, there isn't a decaf version, so I prefer to make this a lunchtime treat.

1 tsp matcha

40ml (1½fl oz) hot water, approximately 75–80°C (165–176°F)

A scoop of softened vanilla ice cream, around 50g (2oz)

Make the matcha using the hot water, following the method on page 49.

Add a scoop of vanilla ice cream to a cup, bowl, or heatproof serving glass. Pour the hot matcha over the top and serve straight away.

MATCHA BASQUE CHEESECAKE

PREP: 20 MINUTES + COOLING • COOK: 30–40 MINUTES • SERVES 8–10

In terms of contemporary culinary classics, matcha and Basque cheesecakes feel like they share a similar space. While matcha has been around a lot longer, both the drink and the cheesecake are local specialities that escaped their borders and came to dominate the global dining scene. The first Basque cheesecake was made in a pintxo bar in San Sebastián in the 1980s. Chef Santi Rivera wanted to create a cheesecake that melted in the mouth. The burnt Basque cheesecake was the triumphant result of all his experiments. To make sure your matcha-flavoured version has that famously light, silky texture, take the cheesecake out of the oven while it's still wobbly in the middle and let it cool for a few hours at room temperature. You'll be rewarded with a cheesecake that's velvety-soft, custardy, and rich.

- 700g (1lb 8oz) full-fat cream cheese, room temperature
- 200ml (7fl oz) double cream
- 150ml (5fl oz) soured cream
- 250g (9oz) caster sugar
- A pinch of salt
- 4 large eggs
- 2 tbsp cornflour
- 2 tbsp matcha

Preheat your oven to 230°C/Fan 210°C/450°F/Gas 8. Line the base and sides of a deep, 23cm (9in) round cake tin with baking paper, leaving a generous amount of paper overhanging the sides to help lift the cheesecake out of the tin later.

Add the cream cheese to a large mixing bowl. Beat with an electric mixer on its lowest setting until smooth. Beat in the double cream and soured cream. Add the sugar with a pinch of salt and slowly beat until the sugar has dissolved.

Beat in the eggs, one at a time. Scoop 4 tablespoons of the mix into a separate bowl. Add the cornflour to it and sift in the matcha. Stir to combine them, then pour the cornflour–matcha mix back into the main bowl. Beat until smoothly combined.

Pour the cheesecake mixture into the tin. Bang the tin on your kitchen counter a few times to burst any bubbles, then bake for 30–40 minutes, or until the top is well browned, the sides are set, but the middle is still molten and shimmies when you gently shake the tin.

Take the cheesecake out of the oven and let it cool at room temperature for 3–4 hours until the middle looks firmer. Use the paper to lift the cheesecake out of the tin. Transfer to a serving plate and serve warm, or chill in the fridge overnight before serving.

The cheesecake can be kept in the fridge for up to 5 days.

MATCHA ICE CREAM

PREP: 30 MINUTES + OVERNIGHT FREEZING • COOK: 5–8 MINUTES • SERVES 4–6

The most refreshing way to enjoy matcha, this scoopable ice cream combines an intense hit of green tea with the indulgent richness of dairy. The base for the ice cream is a homemade custard made with double cream and full-fat milk cooked with egg yolks and sugar to make a lusciously thick sauce. It's flavoured with both matcha and vanilla, a combination I love. The naturally sweet marshmallow and caramel richness of vanilla is the perfect foil for matcha's biting green aromas and oceanic minerality. They are mouthwatering mixed together, especially in this ice cream. Serve it by itself or turn it into a sundae by piling it up in a dish with scoops of chocolate and vanilla ice cream, some whipped cream, chocolate sauce, and flaked almonds.

- 250ml (9fl oz) double cream
- 200ml (7fl oz) full-fat milk
- A pinch of salt
- 2 tbsp matcha
- 4 egg yolks
- 200g (7oz) caster sugar
- 2 tsp vanilla extract
- Mint sprigs, to garnish

Pour the cream and milk into a pan. Add a pinch of salt and sift in the matcha. Set on a medium heat and gently warm, whisking occasionally, until the cream comes to the boil. Take off the heat and set aside to cool.

Slide the egg yolks into a mixing bowl. Add the sugar and vanilla. Use electric beaters to beat them together until they're pale. This may take a few minutes. Slowly trickle the matcha–cream mixture into the egg yolks, beating constantly with the electric beaters.

Pour the mixture into your ice cream maker and follow the manufacturer's instructions to churn. If you don't have an ice cream mixer, pour the mixture into a freezerproof tub and freeze until solid, stirring with a fork every 2 hours to break up any ice crystals until the ice cream is smooth.

To serve, take the ice cream out of the fridge and let it soften at room temperature for 5–10 minutes. Serve in scoops with mint sprigs.

COCONUT & MATCHA ICE POPS

PREP: 15 MINUTES + OVERNIGHT FREEZING • COOK: NIL • MAKES 6

When it's so hot an iced drink won't be enough to cool you down, make these Coconut & Matcha Ice Pops. Essentially, they are frozen matcha lattes on a stick – a combination of coconut milk, matcha, and simple syrup with a squeeze of lime juice to brighten all the flavours. It might seem like a lot of simple syrup in proportion to the coconut milk, but foods taste less sweet the colder they are, so you need more syrup than you think. It also helps to give the coconut milk a softer, more biteable texture. There's a recipe opposite so you can make your own simple syrup, or you can normally find it in the cocktail ingredients section at your local supermarket.

1 tbsp matcha
60ml (2½fl oz) hot water, approximately 75–80°C (165–176°F)
400ml (14fl oz) tin of full-fat coconut milk
100ml (4fl oz) simple syrup (shop-bought, or see recipe opposite)
Juice of 1 lime
A few pinches of chia seeds

Make the matcha with the hot water, following the method on page 49. Set aside to cool.

Give the tin of coconut milk a good shake to mix the coconut cream and water together, then pour into a mixing bowl. Pour in the simple syrup and the matcha. Squeeze in the lime juice. Whisk together to combine.

Sprinkle a few pinches of chia seeds into the base of a set of 6 lolly moulds. Pour the coconut and matcha mixture into the moulds, fix ice lolly sticks in place, and freeze overnight until set.

To release the ice pops from the moulds, dip the moulds briefly in warm water, then carefully pull out the lollies. You can store the lollies in the moulds or in a freezerproof tub, separated by sheets of greaseproof paper. The ice pops will keep in the freezer for up to 3 months.

HOW TO MAKE SIMPLE SYRUP

Tip 75g (3oz) caster sugar into a small pan. Pour in 75ml (3fl oz) water. Set on a high heat and bring to the boil. Turn the heat down and simmer for 2 minutes. Take off the heat and set aside to cool completely. The simple syrup will keep in a sterilized jar or bottle (see page 108) in the fridge for up to 1 month.

INDEX

Page references in *italics* indicate images.

Camellia sinensis 6, 8, 15
chadōgu (tools) 28, 29, *29*
chaji (tea event) 26, 27
chakai (tea gathering) 26, 27, 30–31
chasen (tea whisk) 18, 21, 28, 29, 34, 38, 48, *48*, 49, 50, 51, 57
chashaku (tea scoop) 21, 28, 38, 48, *48*, 49, 50, 51
chawan (tea bowl) 21, 27, 28, 29, 30, 48, *48*, 49, 50, 51, 57

eighty-eighth day, or '*hachiju hachiya*' 13
Eisai (Buddhist priest) 33, 34; '*Kissa yōjōki*' 34

ichibancha ('first tea') 8, 10

Jukō, Murata 35, 36, 37, 38–9

Kakuzo, Okakura 12, 13
Kamakura Period (1185–1333) 33

L-theanine 8, 15, 16, 18, 54

matcha
 classification 6
 colour of 6, 8, 10, 39, 44
 cultivated varieties (cultivars) 11–12, 43
 equipment 48–9, *48*
 finding perfect 41–44
 flavour extras, matcha latte 46
 functional extras, matcha latte 47
 growth and harvest 6–9, *6*, *7*, *8*, *9*, 11, 12, 44
 health and 7, 8, 14–20, 39
 heritage of 21–31, *23*, *24*, *29*
 history of 32–9, *32*, *39*
 making 48–61, *48*, *50–51*
 making space for 19
 milling 43
 mind, benefits for 18–19
 packaging 10, 41
 pink and blue 45–6, *45*, *46*
 preparing 49–51, *50–51*
 producers 42–3
 recipes 52–175
 regions/locations of growth 7, *7*, 42
 smell 44
 storing 44–5
 term 35
 texture 44

meditation/mindfulness 18, 19–20, 33, 34, 35, 39
Minamoto no Sanetomo 34
Muromachi Period (1336–1573) 35–6
nibancha (second harvest) 9

Recipes 52–175
 Drinks 54–90
 Breakfasts 92–115
 Baking 116–155
 Desserts 156–175

Sakaisenke 37–8
sanbancha (third harvest) 9
san senke (three 'sen' houses) 37
Sen no Rikyū 18, 21, 27, 31, 35, 36, 37, 38
Shoshitsu XV 19
sieve 48, 49
Suga, Taeko 19
syrups 46–7, *47*

tea ceremony 8, 19, 20–29, *24*, 36, 37, 38, 49
tencha 7, 8, 9, 10, 12, 42, 43

Uji, Japan 7, 33, 35, 42

yonbancha (fourth harvest)